AIMING FOR PROFICIENCY IN SPANISH

Patricia A. Lennon

Douglas E. Moore

Language Consultant: Margaret Fernández

 **Proficiency Press Co.**

18 Lucille Avenue
Elmont, NY 11003

Foreign Language Books by Master Teachers for Master Teachers

1-879279-04-5

Cover Design by Martin Carrichner's Design Sense

Other books by Proficiency Press Co. :

C'est Ton Tour Aiming for Proficiency in French
Te Toca a Ti   Aiming for Proficiency in Spanish
Du Bist Dran Aiming for Proficiency in German
The Foreign Language Teacher's Handbook: Aiming for Proficiency in French
The Foreign Language Teacher's Handbook: Aiming for Proficiency in Italian
The Foreign Language Teacher's Handbook: Aiming for Proficiency in German
The Foreign Language Teacher's Handbook: Aiming for Proficiency in Spanish
Sigueme Aiming for Proficiency in Spanish
Suivez-moi Aiming for Proficiency in French
Seguimi Aiming for Proficiency in Italian *(Available Spring 1995)*

Copyright © 1994, 1990 by Proficiency Press Co. All rights reserved
No part of this book may be reproduced by photostat, microfilm, xerography, or any other means, or incorporated into any information retrieval system, electronic or mechanical, without permission from the publisher.

All inquiries should be addressed to:
Proficiency Press Co.
18 Lucille Avenue
Elmont, New York 11003

Printed in the U.S.A.

PREFACE

IT'S YOUR TURN

TE TOCA A TI is an innovative approach to foreign language study.

Listening, reading, writing and speaking activities are presented in a uniquely enjoyable manner. The emphasis is on real-life situations in which students interact in Spanish

Each chapter focuses on a practical topic beginning with clearly defined aims for the student.

Included in **TE TOCA A TI** are stimulating communicative sections designed to spark the students' interest and imagination:

>   LISTENING
>   CONVERSATION WITH A PARTNER
>   READING
>   WRITING
>   SPEAKING SITUATIONS
>   PUZZLES

TE TOCA A TI is part of a total program which is also comprised of <u>The Foreign Language Teacher's Handbook: Aiming For Proficiency in Spanish</u>. This <u>Teacher's Handbook</u> presents: core vocabulary, a testing program and supplementary activities for each topic.

Together the <u>Teacher's Handbook</u> and the students' books provide a modern program of basic foreign language instruction.

ACKNOWLEDGMENTS

We are grateful to the following people for their assistance in the creation and publication of this book:

For their invaluable help and support: Mr. David Kreutz, Mr. Richard Hoppenhauer. Mr. Walter Kleinmann, Mrs. Madeline Hendrix

For their technical assistance: Mr. Vincent DiMartino, Ms. Carin Cristodero, Ms. Margaret Fernandez

We would like to give special thanks to our families for their understanding and support.

TABLE OF CONTENTS

PERSONAL IDENTIFICATION..........1

FAMILY LIFE 13

HOUSE AND HOME..................27

EDUCATION.......................35

COMMUNITY AND NEIGHBORHOOD......45

MEAL TAKING FOOD/DRINK..........57

SHOPPING........................71

HEALTH AND WELFARE..............81

PHYSICAL ENVIRONMENT............91

EARNING A LIVING................105

LEISURE.........................118

PUBLIC SERVICES.................129

TRAVEL..........................139

PERSONAL IDENTIFICATION

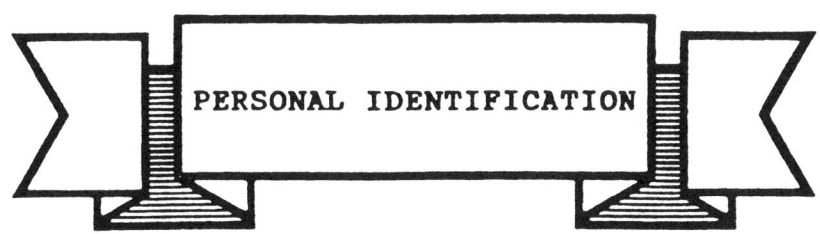

AIMS

You will be able to...

- greet others and introduce yourself.

- provide and obtain identification information: name, birth date, nationality, age, telephone number, address, etc.

- give a description of the personality and physical appearance of yourself and others.

- express interests (likes and dislikes).

PERSONAL IDENTIFICATION

LISTENING

PART A.

Listen carefully to the descriptions. Each description will be read twice. Decide if the following statements are **true** or **false**, based on what you hear.

Paragraph 1

TRUE   **FALSE**

____   ____   1. Pedro is short and skinny.

____   ____   2. Pedro is good-looking.

____   ____   3. He has blue eyes and black hair.

____   ____   4. He lives in Venezuela.

Paragraph 2

____   ____   1. Teresa was born in July.

____   ____   2. Teresa has green eyes and black hair.

____   ____   3. She is South American.

____   ____   4. She is tall and skinny.

Part B.

Listen carefully to each description that will be read to you twice and write the name of the person next to the picture being described.

Ángela   Señora Ramírez   Pablo   Juan   Luisa

a _____

b _____

c _____

d _____

e _____

LISTENING   PERSONAL IDENTIFICATION

PART C.

Listen carefully to the questions that will be read twice.
Choose the correct response from below and write it on the
line provided.

1._____
2._____
3._____
4._____
5._____

En Santo Domingo

Bien, gracias

555-3210

El cuatro de julio

Diego Ortega

SPEAKING

CONVERSATION WITH A PARTNER

PART A.

Let's find out about your partner's likes and dislikes by
asking questions about the activities in the list below.
Put a check in the appropriate column according to his/her answer.

  example: You: ¿Te gusta estudiar?

          Your partner: Sí, me gusta estudiar o
                        No me gusta estudiar.

ACTIVIDAD	Sí	No
1. leer		
2. escuchar la radio		
3. bailar		
4. cantar		
5. hacer la tarea		
6. viajar		
7. trabajar		
8. mirar la televisión		
9. dormir		
10. jugar a los deportes		

CONVERSATION WITH A PARTNER   PERSONAL IDENTIFICATION

PART B.

Your teacher has asked you to help her with a survey about the people in your class. Find out the following information about four of your classmates. Write the information on the lines below.

Ask about: 1. Full name   2. Date of birth
           3. Place of birth 4. Nationality

Use these questions:

　　　　1. ¿Cómo te llamas?

　　　　2. ¿Cuándo naciste?

　　　　3. ¿Dónde naciste?

　　　　4. ¿Cuál es tu nacionalidad?

Persona A　　　　　　　　　　　**Persona B**

1._____　　　1._____

2._____　　　2._____

3._____　　　3._____

4._____　　　4._____

Persona C　　　　　　　　　　　**Persona D**

1. _____　　　1. _____

2. _____　　　2. _____

3. _____　　　3. _____

4. _____　　　4. _____

CONVERSATION WITH A PARTNER   PERSONAL IDENTIFICATION

CONVERSATION WITH A PARTNER   PERSONAL IDENTIFICATION

PART C.

UNA ENCUESTA

You would like to find out about the people in your class. Conduct a survey to learn more about them by asking questions and recording the names of the people who answer "yes". Once you record a "yes" answer, move on to another person.

Ask: ¿Eres tú <u>inteligente</u>?   Write the names of the people who answer "yes" on the line.

Find someone who is...

NOMBRE

inteligente	_____
atlético,a	_____
débil	_____
fuerte	_____
perezoso,a	_____
responsable	_____
estudioso,a	_____

PERSONAL IDENTIFICATION

READING

PART A.

This is an ID card for a new student in your home room. Read the information so that you will know something about him when he enters.

IDENTIFICATION CARD
CARNET DE IDENTIFICACIÓN

FIRMA _José Luis López_

PROFESIÓN _estudiante_

ESTATURA _1,6 metros_

COLOR DE OJOS _azules_

COLOR DE PELO _castaño_

INFORMACIÓN PERSONAL

APELLIDO _López_

NOMBRE _José Luis_

FECHA DE NACIMIENTO _5/9/75_

LUGAR DE NACIMIENTO _Madrid_

DIRECCIÓN _Calle Vega 31_

CIUDAD _Salamanca_

NACIONALIDAD _español_

Answer the questions in Spanish based on the ID card above.

1. ¿Cómo se llama? _____
2. ¿Cuándo nació? _____
3. ¿Dónde nació? _____
4. ¿Dónde vive? _____
5. ¿Cuál es su profesión? _____
6. ¿De qué color son sus ojos? _____
7. ¿De qué color es su pelo? _____

READING

PART B.   PERSONAL IDENTIFICATION

Read the following Personal ads, and then answer the
questions that follow in English.

Me llamo **Ana.** Soy peruana. Tengo catorce años. Soy estudiante. Yo soy rubia y tengo ojos pardos. Me gusta bailar, cantar y escuchar música. Yo soy amable, estudiosa, romántica y simpática.

Me llamo **Luis**. Soy americano. Tengo trece años y soy estudiante. Tengo pelo rubio, ojos verdes, y soy alto y delgado. Me gusta leer, estudiar y escuchar música. Yo soy guapo, inteligente y cómico.

Me llamo **Rosamaría.** Soy inglesa. Yo tengo quince años. Soy estudiante. Tengo pelo negro y ojos verdes. Me gusta ir de compras, hablar por teléfono y no me gusta la escuela. Soy bonita y simpática.

Me llamo **Tomás.** Soy alemán. Tengo trece años. Soy alto, rubio y tengo ojos verdes. Me gusta mirar la telévisión y cantar. Yo soy inteligente, simpático y cariñoso.

1. Who likes to study? _____
2. Who is the oldest? _____
3. Who has black hair? _____
4. What nationality is Tomas? _____
5. Who likes to go shopping? _____
6. Who likes to dance? _____
7. What does Luis look like? _____
   _____
8. Who is funny? _____

PERSONAL IDENTIFICATION

WRITING

Part A.

You would like to order a magazine as a present for your pen pal in Argentina. Fill out the order form below. Give information about yourself and your friend.

RECIBE EN TU CASA

12 ejemplares
por solo $15

¡SUBSCRIBETE HOY!

Esta oferta es válida

SOLO PARA NUEVAS SUBSCRIPCIONES

Hacer cheque o giro postal a nombre de:

EDITORIAL AMERICA, S.A.

REGALE 1 AÑO POR $15.00.
Por favor envíe, como regalo de Navidad, una subscripción anual de TU MÚSICA Y MÚSICOS a las personas abajo nombradas

1er. regalo:

Nombre: _____

Dirección _____

Ciudad _____ Estado ____

AHORRESE UN 30%

Mi nombre _____

Dirección _____

Ciudad _____ Estado _____

Le ajunto cheque por $ _____ por _____ subscripciones

Envíeme la cuenta por $ _____ por _____ subscripciones

Cargar a mi   VISA   MASTERCARD   número _____

Firma: _____

Su primer ejemplar sera puesto en el correo dentro de ocho semanas.

PERSONAL IDENTIFICATION

WRITING

PART B.

Your friend from Puerto Rico is coming to spend a week at your house. Make a list in Spanish of five activities you are planning to do while he/she is visiting with you.

PART C.

You have just become pen pals with a student in Spain. Write a note of about 5 sentences in which you tell about yourself. Include: a personal description of your physical appearance and your personality. Also mention some of your likes and dislikes.

El saludo (Salutation):   Querido,a

La despedida (Closing):   Atentamente,

_____ fecha

SALUDO

DESPEDIDA

WRITING

PART D.

PERSONAL IDENTIFICATION

You are planning a trip to Spain this summer and must fill out an information form for your passport. Give all the information about yourself that is requested in Spanish.

FORMULARIO PARA UN PASAPORTE			
APELLIDO	NOMBRE	SEGUNDO NOMBRE	
DIRECCIÓN	CIUDAD	ESTADO	CÓDIGO POSTAL
NÚMERO DE TELÉFONO ( )			SEXO V H
FECHA DE NACIMIENTO día fecha mes año			
CIUDAD DE NACIMIENTO		ESTADO	PAÍS
NOMBRE DE PADRE	NOMBRE DE SOLTERA DE LA MADRE		
COLOR DE PELO	COLOR DE OJOS	ESTATURA	
FIRMA	FECHA DE HOY		

CRUCIGRAMA

PERSONAL IDENTIFICATION

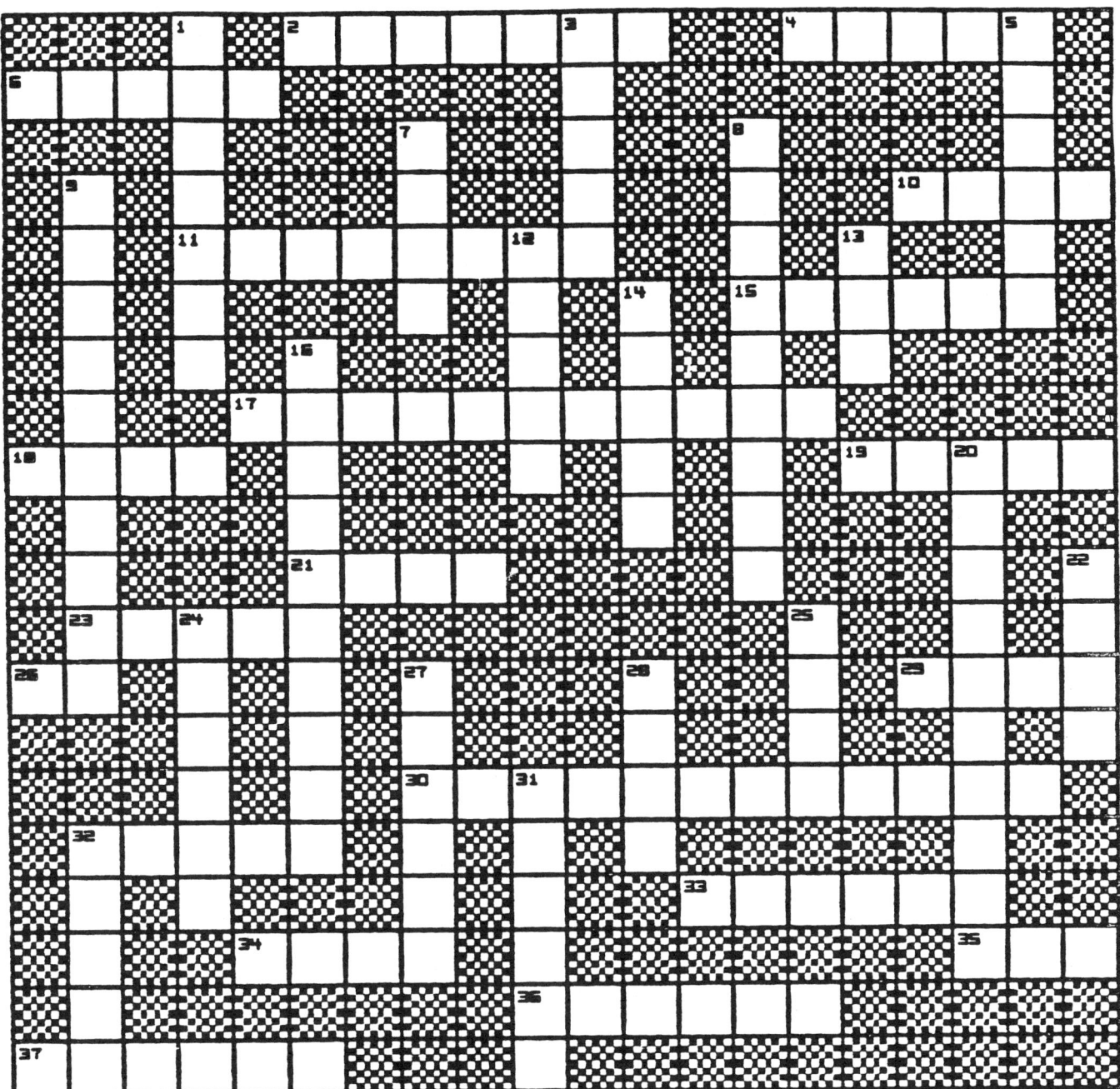

ACROSS CLUES

2. I like
4. no es viejo
6. _____ al tenis
10. estoy _____
11. last name
15. town
17. smart
18. ¿Qué tal?
19. date
21. U.S.A.
23. silly (fem)
26. I
29. no es bajo
30. Soy norteamericano
32. no soy flaco
33. state
34. bad (fem)
35. I'm
36. so-so
37. no es rubio

DOWN CLUES

1. brown
3. no es inteligente (masc)
5. ¿Cuál es tu _____ de teléfono?
7. ¿De qué color tiene el _____?
8. no es antipático
9. fecha de _____ (birth)
12. no es fuerte
13. no es guapo
14. no es malo
16. mean
20. birthday!
22. Cuántos _____ tienes?
24. name
25. blue
27. no es fea
28. Tengo _____ verdes
31. city
32. no es feo

SPEAKING SITUATIONS

PERSONAL IDENTIFICATION

In pairs, prepare the conversations by playing the roles indicated in the situations.

> You are in the local bank. Talk to the teller and give him/her the information he/she needs to open your new account.

> You would like to introduce your friend to a boy/girl you think he/she would like. Persuade your friend to meet this person.

> You and your best friend are discussing the qualities you want in an ideal boyfriend/girlfriend.

> You are talking to a new student from Venezuela. It is his/her first day in your school. Introduce yourselves to each other. Find out all you can about each other.

FAMILY LIFE

You will be able to ...

- identify members of the family.

- discuss daily activities.

- describe the members of your family.

- read and fill out forms and announcements about the family.

- discuss what your family likes to do.

PART A.   FAMILY LIFE

LISTENING

Look at the picture of the Gonzalez family tree. Listen carefully to the questions about the family that will be read twice.

Write the name of the person being described on the line.

1. _____
2. _____
3. _____
4. _____
5. _____

14

LISTENING

FAMILY LIFE

PART B.

Continue to look at the family tree. Listen carefully to each statement read twice about the González family. Determine whether the relationships of the following pairs of people are **true or false.** Check the appropriate box below.

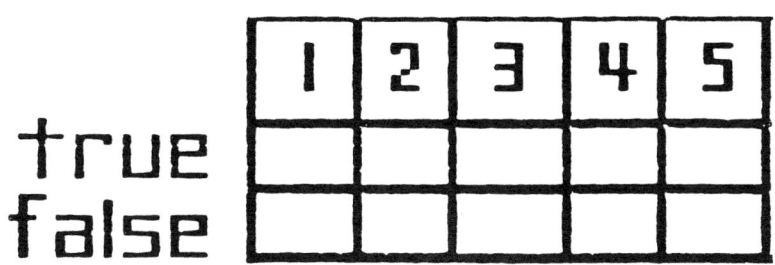

PART C.

Juan is describing members of his family. Listen carefully to each statement that will be read to you twice. Can you identify whom he is describing? Write the letter of your choice in the box.

A. Mi abuelo   B. Mi abuela   C. Mi madre

D. Mi tío   E. Mi padre   F. Mi hermana

LISTENING   FAMILY LIFE

PART D.

Listen carefully to the questions that will be read to you twice. Choose the correct response from below and write it in the space provided.

1. _____
2. _____
3. _____
4. _____
5. _____

- Tiene cuarenta años
- Es muy simpático
- Asiste a la universidad
- Se llama María
- No está muy bien

PART E.

Look at the González family tree again. Listen to your teacher read descriptions of Patricia's relationship to different family members twice. Determine who is being described and write the letter of the correct family member in the box.

A. primas   C. abuelos   D. tía
B. tíos   Ch. padre   E. hermanos

FAMILY LIFE

SPEAKING

CONVERSATION WITH A PARTNER

PART A.

Interview your partner to find out about the people in his/her family. Record your partner's answers below.

Ask: Pregúntale: Answer: Contéstale:

1. ¿Cuántas personas hay en tu familia?   _____

2. ¿Cómo se llama tu padre?   _____

3. ¿Cuántos años tiene tu madre?   _____

5. ¿Cuántos hermanos tienes?   _____

6. ¿Tienes animales?   _____

7. ¿Cuántos abuelos tienes?   _____

PART B.

You are about to meet your boyfriend's/girlfriend's parent. You are anxious to make a good impression. To find out more about this person, ask your friend at least **five** of the following questions. Record the answers on the lines.

Escribe la respuesta aquí.

1. ¿Cómo se llama?   _____

2. ¿Cuántos años tiene?   _____

3. ¿De qué color son sus ojos? _____

4. ¿De qué color es su pelo?   _____

5. ¿Qué le gusta hacer?   _____

6. ¿Cómo es su personalidad?   _____

7. ¿Cuál es su nacionalidad?   _____

8. ¿Dónde trabaja?   _____

9. ¿Cómo es?   _____

FAMILY LIFE

CONVERSATION WITH A PARTNER

PART C.

Find out what your partner's family likes to do. Record the favorite activity of each family member.

Pregúntale: ¿Qué le gusta hacer...   Le gusta.....

- a tu madre?   _____
- a tu padre?   _____
- a tu hermano?   _____
- a tu hermana?   _____
- a tu abuelo?   _____
- a tu perro?   _____
- a tu gato?   _____

PART D.

UNA ENCUESTA

Conduct a survey to learn about the families of your classmates. Ask them a question and record the names of the people who answer "yes."

In order to find someone who has these relatives or animals ask:

¿Tienes tú.....?

	Nombre
una hermana	
dos hermanos	
tres abuelos	
cuatro tías (o más)	
muchos primos	
pocos primos	
un perro	
un gato	

READING

PART A.

EL PREMIO DE PADRE DEL AÑO

El señor Pablo Guzmán fue nombrado "El Padre Del Año." El señor Guzmán tiene dos hijos y dos hijas. Su esposa Manuela dice que él siempre es amable y está contento. Pablo es profesor de matemáticas en la escuela secundaria de San Rafael. El es entrenador de un equipo de fútbol de niños y es el líder de un club de jóvenes en su barrio. El también trabaja de voluntario en un hospital en su pueblo. Todos sus vecinos dicen que es simpático y cariñoso.

Now that you have read about el Sr. Guzmán, decide if the following statements are "Verdad" o "Mentira". Write **V or M** on the line.

1. Mr. Guzmán won the lottery. _____

2. Mrs. Guzmán says her husband is a happy person. _____

3. He enjoys being with children. _____

4. He works in a hospital as a doctor. _____

5. His neighbors are fond of him. _____

PART · B   FAMILY LIFE

LA FLORISTA ÁLVAREZ

OFRECE TODA CLASE DE FLORES

Recuerde a su **mamá** en El Día de las Madres
con el regalo más preferido.

el 7 de mayo

Distribuimos sus órdenes a cualquier dirección en este pueblo.

LA FLORISTA ÁLVAREZ
CALLE GRAN VIA 34
TORREMOLINOS
LLAMENOS 23 46 75

Answer these questions in Spanish.

1. ¿Cuál día especial se celebra pronto? _____

2. ¿Para quién es esta fiesta? _____

3. ¿Qué prefiere recibir muchas madres? _____

4. ¿Cual es la fecha de la fiesta? _____

READING

PART C.

We all have our own daily routine that we follow. Read the following list of activities. Then put them in order according to your own preference.

  _____ Me baño/me ducho.

  _____ Me levanto.

  _____ Me desayuno.

  _____ Me voy al colegio.

  _____ Me despierto.

  _____ Me visto.

  _____ Me cepillo los dientes.

  _____ Me cepillo el pelo.

Compare your list to your conversation partner's to see if there are differences.

FAMILY LIFE

WRITING IN SPANISH

PART A.

Your pen pal from Mexico is about to visit you. He wants to know all about your family. Write a note of about 6 sentences in which you describe your family and its members. You may include: names, ages, activities and size of family.

_____
fecha

_____
saludo

_____
_____
_____
_____
_____

_____
despedida
_____

PART B.

Your teacher has asked you about your family. Write a list of four of your family members and a word which describes each person. *Use a different word to describe each person.

_____   _____
_____   _____
_____   _____
_____   _____

FAMILY LIFE

PART C.

You are filling out the U.S. Census. Person #1 is the head of your household. The others are relatives of Person #1 who live in your house. Complete the form by filling in or checking the appropriate boxes.

CUESTIONARIO - EL CENSO DE LOS ESTADOS UNIDOS

PERSONA #1	PERSONA #2	PERSONA #3	PERSONA #4
_____	_____	_____	_____
apellido	apellido	apellido	apellido
_____	_____	_____	_____
nombre	nombre	nombre	nombre
	Si pariente de persona #1	Si pariente de persona #1	Si pariente de persona #1
	esposo ☐	esposo ☐	esposo ☐
	esposa ☐	esposa ☐	esposa ☐
	hijo ☐	hijo ☐	hijo ☐
	hija ☐	hija ☐	hija ☐
	hermano ☐	hermano ☐	hermano ☐
	hermana ☐	hermana ☐	hermana ☐
	padre ☐	padre ☐	padre ☐
	madre ☐	madre ☐	madre ☐

Sexo	Sexo	Sexo	Sexo
V ☐ H ☐	V ☐ H ☐	V ☐ H ☐	V ☐ H ☐
Edad	Edad	Edad	Edad
☐☐	☐☐	☐☐	☐☐
Fecha de nacimiento	Fecha de nacimiento	Fecha de nacimiento	Fecha de nacimiento
___/___/___	___/___/___	___/___/___	___/___/___
día mes año	día mes año	día mes año	día mes año

FAMILY LIFE

MAKE YOUR OWN FAMILY TREE

Make a family tree for one side of your family.
Draw horizontal lines for your grandparents, parents, sisters
and brothers. Then write the names of the family members
on the line and their relationship to you in Spanish below
the line.

** FAMILY **

```
H F A M I L I A D R D D
R J Q H I J O P T S P M
A B H S E T N E I R A F
B I A B U E L O I D P T
U S G E U T F M R A U I
E A E S P D O E V O X O
L B S P A D R I N O M V
A U P O A O V E R D A M
V E O S W D S P T J L C
C L S A S R R P Y Q Z F
B O O Y F Y Q E Y R S L
H H E R M A N O F X O H
```

Write the Spanish for each of the words below. Then find them in the puzzle.

1. FAMILY _____
2. HUSBAND _____
3. MOTHER _____
4. SON _____
5. GRANDMOTHER _____
6. GODFATHER _____
7. RELATIVES _____
8. GREAT GRANDFATHER _____
9. GRANDFATHER _____
10. UNCLE _____
11. FATHER _____
12. COUSIN (M) _____
13. MOTHER _____
14. BROTHER _____
15. WIFE. _____

SPEAKING SITUATIONS

FAMILY LIFE

In pairs, prepare the conversations playing the roles indicated in the situations.

You and a new Spanish-speaking friend are discussing families. Socialize and discuss brothers and sisters

Your school nurse needs information about your family for the Emergency Card. Provide the information.

You want your friend to go out with your brother/sister. Convince him/her by describing your brother/sister.

You are talking to your mother on the phone after meeting your pen pal's family in Spain. Discuss how you feel about the members of his family.

HOUSE AND HOME

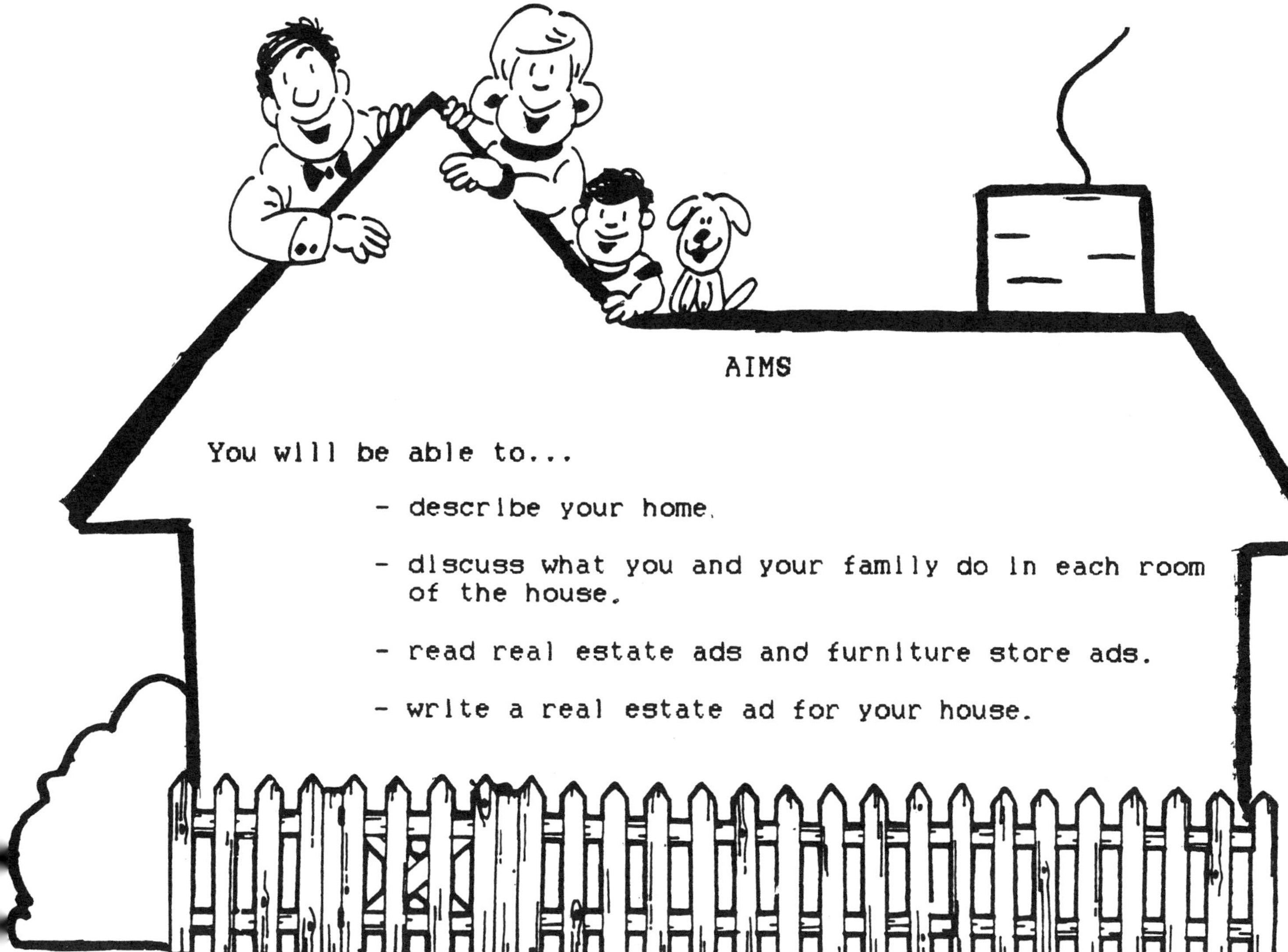

AIMS

You will be able to...

- describe your home.

- discuss what you and your family do in each room of the house.

- read real estate ads and furniture store ads.

- write a real estate ad for your house.

HOUSE AND HOME

LISTENING

PART A.

Pablo is telling you what he does on a typical day. Listen to what he says and decide in which room of the house he does that activity. Each sentence will be read twice. Then write the number of the sentence next to the appropriate picture.

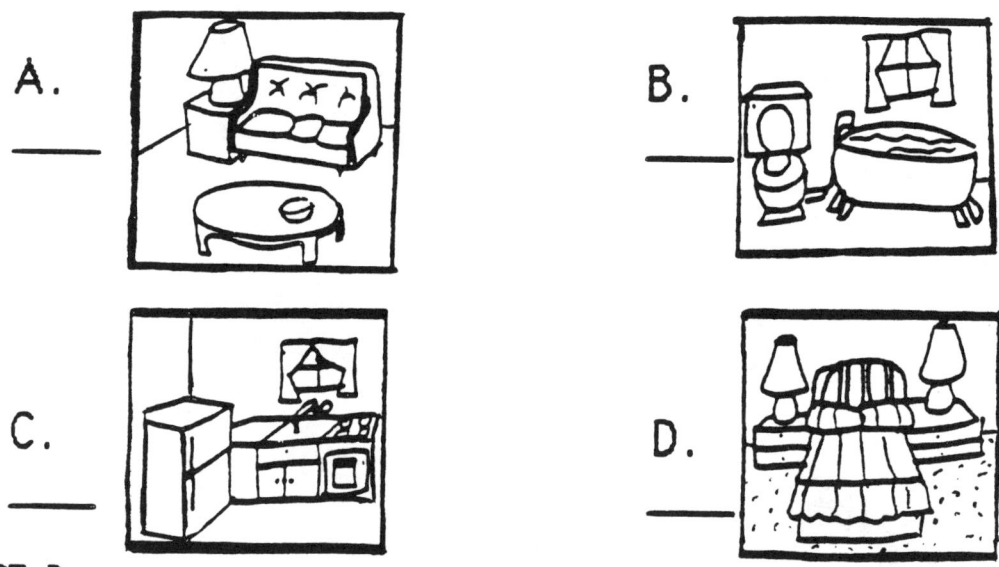

A. ___

B. ___

C. ___

D. ___

PART B.

Teresa is telling you about her house. Decide if what she is telling you is true or false according to the picture. Each statement will be read twice. Place a check in the appropriate box below.

	1	2	3	4	5
TRUE					
FALSE					

CONVERSATION WITH A PARTNER HOUSE AND HOME

SPEAKING

PART A.

You have just moved to a new house that is not completely furnished. Talk with your partner about what furniture there is in each room and what pieces you still need.

Ejemplo: 1. ¿Qué hay en tu <u>cocina</u>?
          2. Hay <u>un refrigerador</u>.
          1. ¿Qué necesitas en tu <u>cocina</u>?
          2. Necesito <u>una estufa</u>.

<u>Useful Expressions</u>

¿Qué hay?
Hay
Necesito

<u>Rooms</u>

la cocina
el baño
la sala
el dormitorio
el comedor

PART B.

You want to sell your summer home in Spain. You decide to go to a real estate agent to help you sell it. One of you will play the role of the client and will describe the house you want to sell. The other student will play the role of the real estate agent and will fill out the form below for your files.

AGENCIA BIENES RAÍCES LÓPEZ

Calle Colón, 23

460010 - Valencia

Tel. (96) 33 02 43

NOMBRE DEL AGENTE_____

NOMBRE DEL CLIENTE_____

_____CASA _____APARTAMENTO _____COMPRAR _____ALQUILAR

LOCALIDAD: _____CIUDAD _____AFUERAS ******************

NÚMERO DE PISOS_____**********************************

NÚMERO DE HABITACIONES_____ NÚMERO DE BAÑOS_____***********

NÚMERO DE DORMITORIOS_____**************************************

GARAJE _____SÍ _____NO
JARDÍN _____SÍ _____NO
PISCINA _____SÍ _____NO
SÓTANO _____SÍ _____NO

HOUSE AND HOME

READING

PART A.

Read the following real estate ads from a Mexican newspaper and answer the questions that follow.

CLASIFICADOS — VIVIENDAS Y BIENES RAICES

A GUADALAJARA Vendo casa, una sala, 3 dormitorios, una chimenea, comedor, 2 baños, jardín grande, garaje. ¡Una ganga! Tel. 331-42-90

B CHIHUAHUA Alquila julio y agosto, da al Río Concho, apartamento, despacho, cocina, baño. Buen Precio. Tel 34-23-12

C ACAPULCO alquilo apartamento 1 dormitorio, amueblado, garaje. A 100 metros de la playa. (21) 555-32-47 (noches solo)

D TIJUANA Vendo apartamento con cocina, despacho, 2 dormitorios, baño, terraza, piscina. $1.500.000 pesos Tel. 32-54-89

1. Where can you rent an apartment for the summer? _____
2. What number must be called in the evenings? _____
3. Which ad features a pool? _____
4. What number would you call if you wanted to buy an apartment? _____
5. Which number would you call to buy a house? _____
6. Which listing has the most bedrooms? _____
7. Which ad has a living room and a dining room? _____
8. Which ad describes an apartment on the water? _____
9. Which phone numbers would you call if you were looking for an apartment to rent? _____
10. Which ad features a fireplace? _____

PART B.   HOUSE AND HOME

While in Spain, you are reading the newspaper and see these furniture store ads. Read them and answer the questions that follow in Spanish.

La Fuente

lávabos
bañeras
duchas
espejos

avda. del Río, 9
28019 - Madrid

Cenicienta

neveras
tostadores
estufas
hornos
microondas
abrelatas

SAGUNTO, 18
28001 - MADRID

Hermanos Hernández

C/ O'Donnell, 67
28006 - Madrid

SOFÁS
MESAS
ESTANTES
LÁMPARAS

todo de nueva moda europea

el Dormilón

CAMAS DE TODA CLASE

COLCHONES   ARMARIOS

Castellana 53
28022 - Madrid

1. ¿Dónde se compran los muebles para el dormitorio?
   _____

2. ¿Para cuál habitación son las cosas en "La Fuente?
   _____

3. ¿Dónde se compran los electrodomésticos para la cocina?
   _____

4. ¿Dónde se compran los muebles para la sala?
   _____

5. ¿Qué se compra en "Hermanos Hernández?
   _____

HOUSE AND HOME

WRITING

PART A.

Let's pretend that you are an interior decorator who is going through a house. In Spanish, make a list of what you need to furnish each room you pass through. List three items for each room.

el dormitorio

_____
_____
_____

el comedor

_____
_____
_____

la sala

_____
_____
_____

el baño

_____
_____
_____

PART B.

You have redecorated your room. Write a letter to your cousin describing what it looks like now in Spanish.

_____
_____
_____
_____
_____

PART C.

Your parents are selling your house. Write the ad you must bring to the local newspaper in Spanish.

_____
_____
_____
_____
_____

CRUCIGRAMA — HOUSE AND HOME

ACROSS CLUES

3. room
7. dining room
8. lamp
9. kitchen
10. den, office
12. fireplace, chimney
16. bathroom
20. refrigerator
21. chair
22. radio
23. curtains
24. toilet
25. bathroom sink
26. garage

DOWN CLUES

1. bedroom
2. door
4. window
5. bedroom
6. backyard, garden
7. bed
11. basement
13. stove
14. china closet
15. kitchen sink
17. television
18. table
19. pool

HOUSE AND HOME
SPEAKING SITUATIONS

In pairs, prepare the conversation playing the roles indicated in the situation.

> You have just moved to a new house. Tell your friend about the house.

> You are looking at an apartment with a real estate agent. Tell him/her what you think about it.

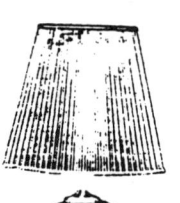

> You are thinking about renting an apartment for the summer. You are on the phone with the owner. Ask him/her about the apartment.

> You would like new furniture for your room. Tell your parent what you want and convince him/her to buy it for you.

EDUCATION

AIMS

You will be able to...

- identify classroom items.
- identify school related activities.
- describe your school, classes and teachers.
- read and fill-in a schedule of classes.
- read and understand a report card.
- tell another student about your classroom, classes, teachers and school activities.

LISTENING EDUCATION

PART A.

Monte Mentiroso is describing his classroom. Listen and decide if the statements you hear are **true** or **false** based on the picture you see. Choose the correct answer and check the appropriate box.

	1	2	3	4	5	6	7	8
true								
false								

EDUCATION

LISTENING

PART B.

As you are walking down a hallway of a high school in Mexico City, you hear some of the teachers speaking to their classes. Decide which classes they are teaching by listening carefully to the statements that will be read to you twice. In the boxes, write the letter of the picture that best illustrates the class being described. There is one extra picture.

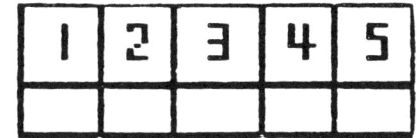

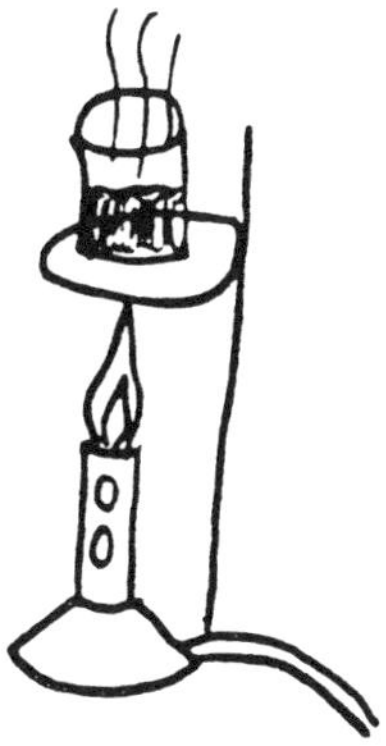

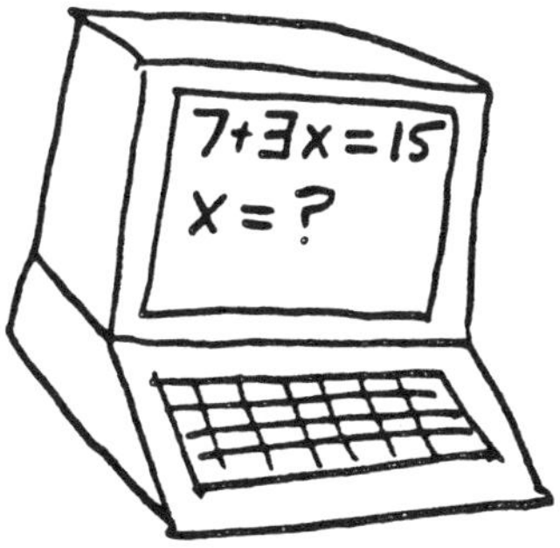

EDUCATION

CONVERSATION WITH A PARTNER

PART A.

Let's find out about your partner's feelings on school subjects and activities. Use the chart to log the answers to the following questions:

1. ¿Te gusta _____? Te gustan _____
   la clase   las clases

2. ¿Cuál es tu nota en la clase?

Clase	Me Gusta	La odio	La Nota
el inglés			
el español			
las matématicas			
la historia			
la tecnología			
las ciencias			
el coro			
el dibujo			

Now ask the following questions and record your partner's answers.

1. ¿Cuál es tu clase favorita? _____
2. ¿Qué haces en esta clase? _____
3. ¿Por qué prefieres esta clase? _____
4. ¿Qué clase es la más difícil? _____
5. ¿Qué clase es la más fácil? _____

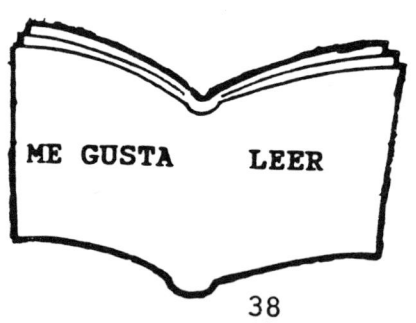
ME GUSTA LEER

38

EDUCATION

CONVERSATION WITH A PARTNER

PART B.

EL HORARIO

Fill out the schedule below for your conversation partner. You must find out all the information needed by asking questions. For example: Ask, ¿Cómo te llamas? to fill in the name. Continue asking the appropriate questions about address and other personal information.

Then use the following questions to fill in the schedule of classes.
1. ¿Qué clase tienes el período uno (dos, tres, etc.)?
2. ¿En qué sala tienes la clase?
3. ¿A qué hora es la clase?
4. ¿Cómo se llama el profesor?

COLEGIO SIMÓN BOLÍVAR

HORARIO DE 19___-19___

Nombre y apellido   Número de teléfono

Domicilio   Estado   Código Postal

PERÍODO	ASIGNATURA/CLASE	SALA	HORA	PROFESOR/A
1				
2				
3				
4				
5				
6				
7				
8				
9				

EDUCATION

READING

PART A.

Manuel has just received his report card. Read it. Then answer the questions below in Spanish.

INSTITUTO Dr. JOSÉ RIVERA

Nombre *Manuel Olvedo* Grado *Tercero*
Maestro *Sr. Feliciano*

Progreso Escolar   1er. PERÍODO

Materia	Nota	
Inglés	8	Hace buen trabajo
Matemáticas Álgebra	7.5	Debe estudiar más
Ciencias Naturales	6.5	Aprobado
Español	7	Es perezoso
Historia	8.5	Es buen estudiante
Geografía	9	Excelente
Música	8	Practica cada día
Dibujo	7	Debe practicar
Ausencias	10	
Tardanzas	6	

Firma de los Padres: *Sr. Héctor Olvedo*

---

1. ¿Qué clase prefiere el estudiante? _____
2. ¿Cuál es la nota más alta? _____
3. ¿Cómo es en la clase de español? _____
4. ¿Qué materia debe (should) estudiar más? _____
5. ¿Qué prefiere más, el arte o las ciencias? _____
6. How many days has he been absent? _____

EDUCATION

READING

PART B.

Read this article from the school newspaper.

> EL DEPARTAMENTO DE HISTORIA
> ANUNCIA LA ALUMNA DEL MES
>
> El Señor Charlatán anunció hoy que Cecilia Cerebro es la alumna del mes del departamento de Historia en el Colegio Cristóbal Colón. Cecilia siempre hace la tarea y saca buenas notas. Su profesor, el Señor Charlatán, dice que Cecilia siempre hace la tarea y saca buenas notas en su clase. Ella es muy popular con los otros profesores y los estudiantes y tiene muchos amigos. Cecilia dice que le gusta mucho la historia norteamericana. Ella dice que lee muchos libros sobre la historia de los Estados Unidos y que su profesor es muy estricto pero también es interesante.

Answer the following questions about this article in English.

1. Who is the article about?
   _____

2. Why was this article written about her?
   _____

3. What is the name of the school?
   _____

4. Why did this student receive this honor?
   _____
   _____

5. Who is the teacher?
   _____

EDUCATION

WRITING

PART A.

You are going to school and want to be sure that you have everything you need. Check the contents of your school bag. List five items in Spanish that you need for school.

PART B.

Your teacher has asked you to help her take inventory of the items in the classroom before putting everything away for the summer. Write a list in Spanish of five items in the classroom.

PART C.

Write a note in Spanish to your cousin who lives in New Mexico and speaks Spanish. Tell him/her about your school, your classes, teachers, and what you do in several of your classes.

CRUCIGRAMA — EDUCATION

CROSS CLUES

1. to paint
2. to draw
6. Gym class
10. El profesor escribe en la_____
11. chalk
12. Spanish
14. 23+5x=77
20. computer
21. test
22. pen
23. Dibujo en la clase de _____
24. class
25. grade

DOWN CLUES

1. teacher (masc)
3. Leo un _____
4. Es roja, blanca y azul
5. schedule
7. science
8. paper
9. pencil
12. alumno
13. social studies
15. to learn
16. notebook
17. desk
18. school
19. English

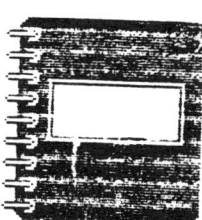

SPEAKING SITUATIONS

EDUCATION

In pairs, prepare the conversations playing the roles indicated in the situations.

> You are talking to an exchange student from Bolivia. Find out what he/she does in five of his/her classes.

> You are in the cafeteria. A new student from Puerto Rico approaches you. Greet him/her and ask about his/her classes.

> You have just received your report card. Discuss it with your Spanish-speaking friends.

> It is August, you and your friend just received schedules for September. Persuade him/her to join your Spanish class.

COMMUNITY AND NEIGHBORHOOD

AIMS

You will be able to...

- describe your town.

- identify buildings and places.

- tell what means of transportation you take to travel.

- give directions from one place to another in your town.

- understand announcements of events taking place in your town.

- write a short note about a town and the activities you do there.

COMMUNITY AND NEIGHBORHOOD

LISTENING

PART A.

Listen to your teacher describe a situation twice. Decide what means of transportation you would use in each situation. Write the letter of the correct answer in the appropriate box.

¿Cómo vas?

PART B. ■ ■ ■ ■   ■ ■ ■ ■

Listen to the descriptions of the different activities that you can do in your town. Decide which one is being described, and write the number next to the picture.

¿Adónde vas?

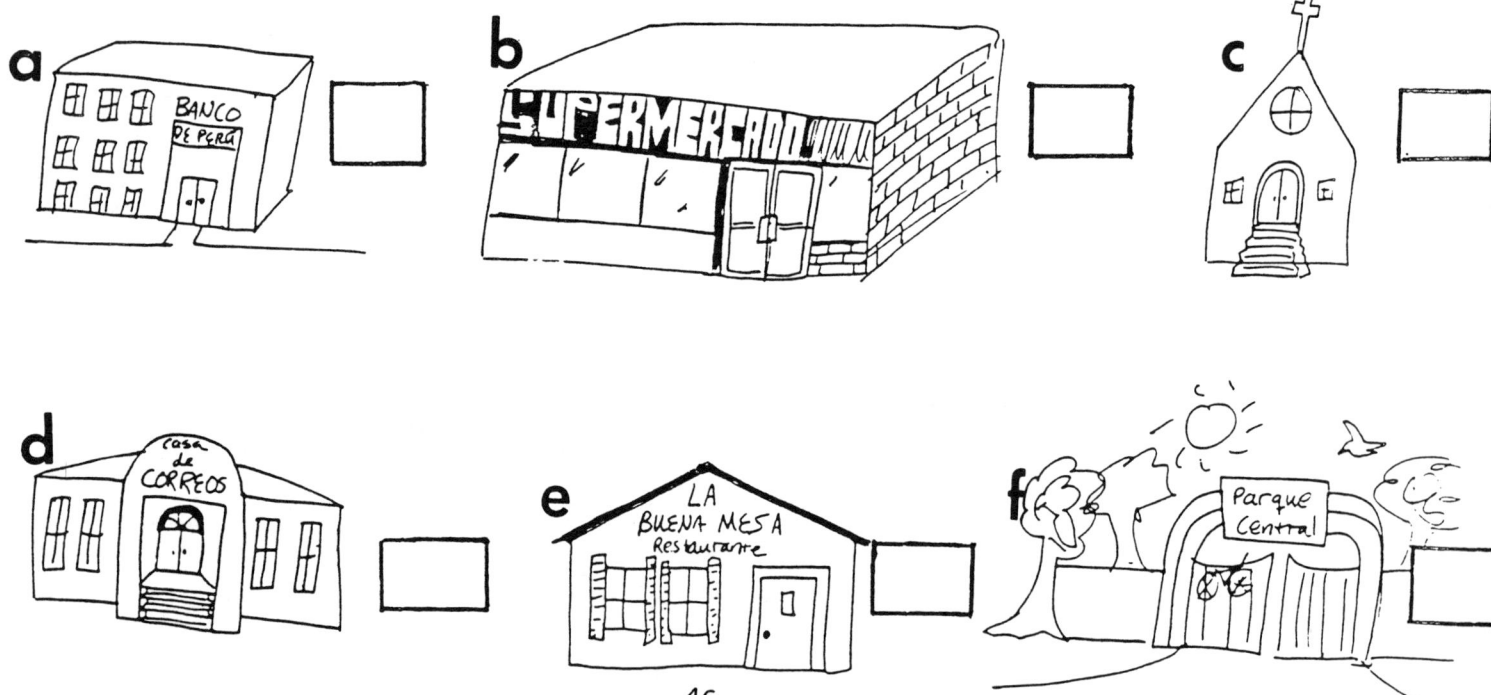

COMMUNITY AND NEIGHBORHOOD

SPEAKING   CONVERSATION WITH YOUR PARTNER

PART A.

Use the following questions to interview your partner in order to find out about his/her town and his/her activities.

¿Cómo se llama tu pueblo? _____

¿Cómo es tu pueblo? _____

¿Qué hay en tu pueblo? _____

¿Qué haces en tu pueblo los domingos? _____

¿Qué haces en tu pueblo los martes? _____

Based on this interview, write a short paragraph about your friend's town. Begin with these words...

   El pueblo de mi amigo es..._____

_____
_____
_____

PART B.

Interview your partner to determine the means of transportation he/she prefers in each situation.

Some samples: AVIÓN   BICICLETA   AUTO   MOTO

A PIE   TAXI   METRO   AUTOBÚS   TREN   BARCO

Ask   ¿Cómo vas?

1. al colegio   Yo voy (en) _____

2. a la casa de un amigo   _____

3. al centro comercial   _____

4. al estadio de béisbol   _____

5. a la casa de tus abuelos   _____

6. al cine   _____

COMMUNITY AND NEIGHBORHOOD

7. a la ciudad   _____

8. a México   _____

9. de un museo al teatro en la
   ciudad   _____

10. por las calles de Bermuda.   _____

PART C.

GIVING DIRECTIONS

While looking at the map, take turns with your partner giving directions from one place in the town to another as suggested below.

1. De la estación de autobús a la Escuela Primaria.

2. De la heladería a la Piscina Municipal.

3. Del estadio de deportes a la universidad.

4. Del parque zoológico al Cine Estrella.

Now take turns with your partner dictating directions to the destination of your choice.

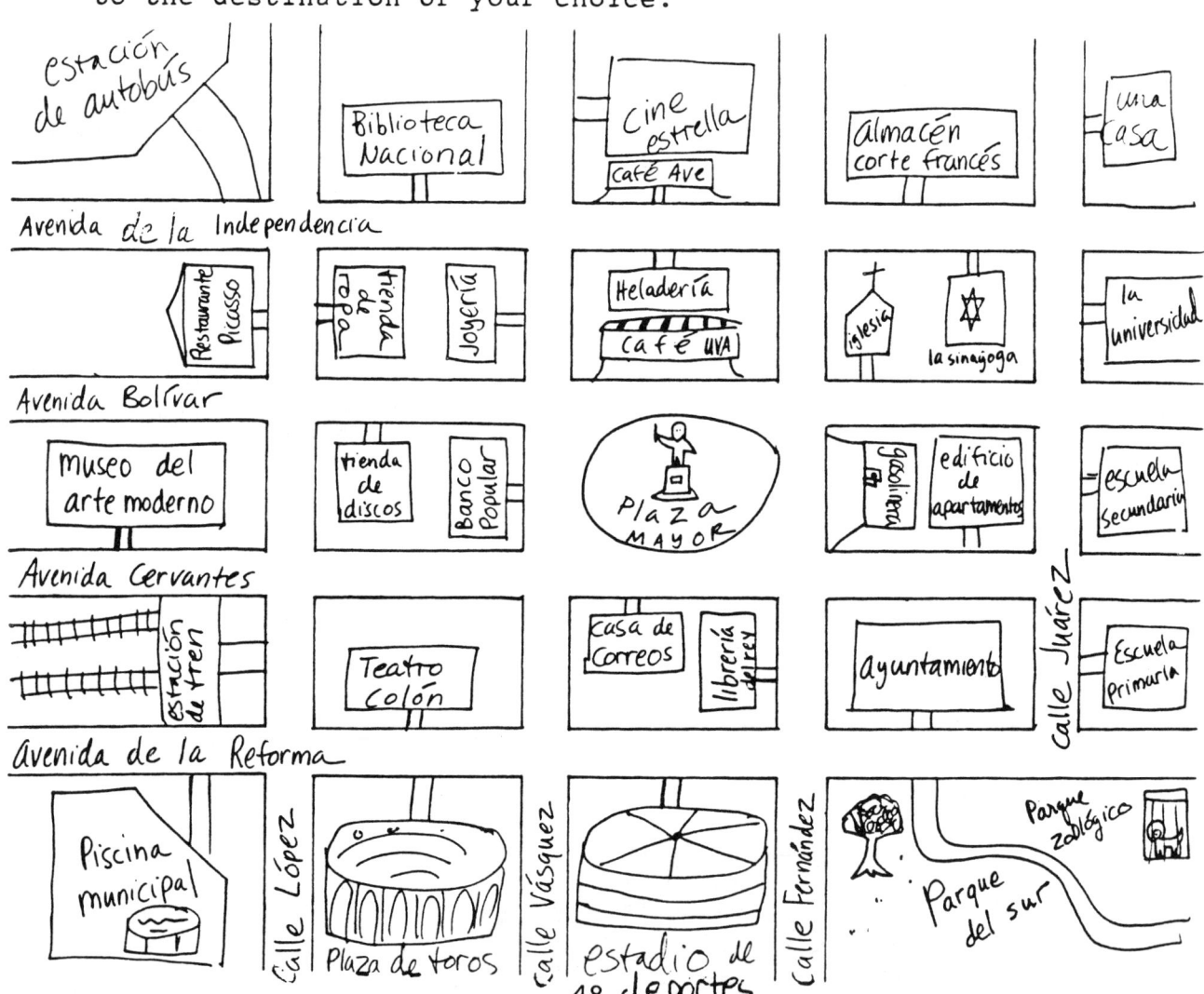

READING   COMMUNITY AND NEIGHBORHOOD

PART A.

Read the following advertisement. Then answer the questions.

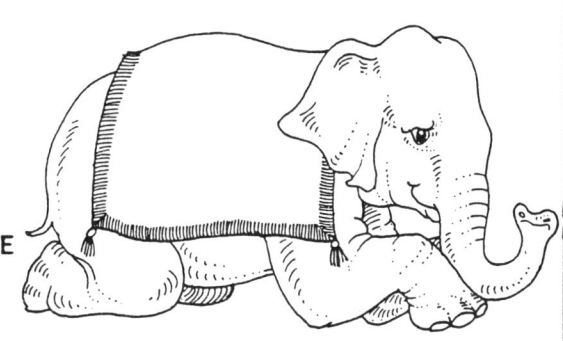

¡ANUNCIANDO!

EL CIRCO

EN EL PUEBLO DE

SAN DIEGO

A LA UNA DE LA TARDE

EL CUATRO DE MAYO

PARA TODA LA FAMILIA

BOLETOS: 400 Y 500 PESOS POR ADULTOS
         300 PESOS POR NIÑOS

Answer the following questions in English.

1. What is taking place in the town? _____
2. What is the name of the town? _____
3. How much is a ticket for a child? _____
4. What date is the performance? _____
5. What time is the performance? _____

Answer the last question in Spanish.

6. ¿Para quién es el circo? _____

PART B.   COMMUNITY AND NEIGHBORHOOD

Read this bulletin about events in the town. Then answer
the questions below.

¿QUÉ PASA
EN EL PUEBLO DE SAN PEDRO?

del 6 al 12 de mayo

6. lunes:

Un concierto en la Plaza Mayor, por Rafael Rafael, a las ocho. Gratis.

7. martes:

Un campeonato de fútbol entre los pueblos de Santa Fe y San Antonio. Empieza a las seis de la tarde.

8. miércoles:

Una conferencia sobre la nutrición por la Doctora Menéndez. Especializa en dietas para las jóvenes. En la Clínica San Martín

9. jueves:

Una reunión de la clase de 1982 en el colegio, Juan Carlos a las 7:30 de la noche.

10. viernes:

Un baile en la Iglesia de San Juan para jóvenes de 15 a 18 años de edad.

11. sábado:

Una feria para jóvenes. Juegos, concursos y mucho de comer. desde las 10 de la mañana hasta las cinco de la tarde en el parque, Bolívar.

12. domingo:

Un debate entre los candidatos para alcalde (mayor) de San Pedro, en el colegio, Francisco Rivera, a las 7 de la noche.

Indicate where you would go in the following situations.
Write the number of the day on the line to the left.

_____ A. ¿Adónde vas por información sobre la buena comida para las jóvenes?

_____ B. Tú quieres ir a un festival.

COMMUNITY AND NEITHBORHOOD

_____ C. Tú tienes interés en los políticos de tu pueblo.

_____ D. A ti te gustan los deportes mucho.

_____ E. Tus amigos quieren practicar algunos nuevos pasos de la salsa y merengue.

_____ F. Tu cantante favorito viene a tu pueblo esta semana.

PART C.

You are on vacation in Spain. You have received this ticket for an upcoming event from your travel agent. Answer the **true/false** questions below.

_____ 1. This ticket is for the national sport of Spain.

_____ 2. It occurs on Saturday.

_____ 3. The tier you will sit on is 8.

_____ 4. The number of the seat is 2.000.

_____ 5. The row is 16.

_____ 6. The time of the performance is 6pm.

_____ 7. The date is June 18.

_____ 8. You are sitting in the sun.

51

COMMUNITY AND NEIGHBORHOOD

WRITING

PART A.

¡UN CONCURSO ACERCA DE TU PUEBLO!

Nueva Vallarta is a new resort town by the beach. Make an illustrated ad advertising this town. Include written information about the town and its activities.

WRITING

COMMUNITY AND NEIGHBORHOOD

PART B.

Your friend is coming to visit you. Make a list in Spanish of four places you would like to go with him/her in your town.

_____   _____

_____   _____

PART C.

Write directions for your friend from school to your house in Spanish.

_____

_____

_____

PART D.

Your pen pal is coming to visit you soon. Write him/her a note telling about your town in Spanish.

_____

_____

_____

_____

COMMUNITY AND NEIGHBORHOOD

CRUCIGRAMA

ACROSS CLUES

2. A place to swim
4. The center of town
5. To walk
7. A place to read
10. A place to eat and drink
12. A car
14. Your community
16. A movie house
17. The store
18. A train
19. A place to buy food
22. A place to play sports
23. A place of worship

DOWN CLUES

1. A place to see plays.
3. A pack animal of Peru.
6. The subway
8. To go shopping
9. A synagogue
11. A plane
12. A steet
13. A place to dine.
15. A place to save money.
20. The bullfight
21. A place to swim

SPEAKING SITUATIONS

COMMUNITY AND NEIGHBORHOOD

In pairs, prepare the conversations playing the roles indicated in the situations.

You are being interviewed by a member of a committee that is looking for the best neighborhood in your county. Tell this person about your neighborhood. Include its best aspects.

Your uncle from California is transferred to your town. Tell your cousins the activities that are offered in your neighborhood.

You are on a plane and meet an immigrant from Argentina. Try to convince him/her to settle in your neighborhood.

You are speaking to the mayor of your town at a village meeting. Tell him/her why you like living in your town.

PART B.   COMMUNITY AND NEIGHBORHOOD

Read this bulletin about events in the town. Then answer
the questions below.

¿QUÉ PASA EN EL PUEBLO DE SAN PEDRO?

del 6 al 12 de mayo

6. lunes:

Un concierto en la Plaza Mayor, por Rafael Rafael, a las ocho. Gratis.

7. martes:

Un campeonato de fútbol entre los pueblos de Santa Fe y San Antonio. Empieza a las seis de la tarde.

8. miércoles:

Una conferencia sobre la nutrición por la Doctora Menéndez. Especializa en dietas para las jóvenes. En la Clínica San Martín

9. jueves:

Una reunión de la clase de 1982 en el colegio, Juan Carlos a las 7:30 de la noche.

10. viernes:

Un baile en la Iglesia de San Juan para jóvenes de 15 a 18 años de edad.

11. sabado:

Una feria para jóvenes. Juegos, concursos y mucho de comer. desde las 10 de la mañana hasta las cinco de la tarde en el parque, Bolívar.

12. domingo:

Un debate entre los candidatos para alcalde (mayor) de San Pedro, en el colegio, Francisco Rivera, a las 7 de la noche.

Indicate where you would go in the following situations.
Write the number of the day on the line to the left.

_____A. ¿Adónde vas por información sobre la buena comida para las jóvenes?

_____B. Tú quieres ir a un festival.

MEAL TAKING FOOD AND DRINK

AIMS

You will be able to ...

- understand which meal is being eaten according to the food mentioned.

- identify the food in the different food groups and meals.

- find out the likes and dislikes of another person with regard to the foods learned.

- identify the silverware and other items used to set a table.

- order food in a restaurant.

- read a menu and ads for food and restaurants.

- write a shopping list and note about shopping for food.

MEAL TAKING
FOOD AND DRINK

LISTENING

PART A.

Listen carefully to the passages that will be read to you twice. Then decide which meal is being described and write the letter of the correct answer in the appropriate box. One answer will be used twice.

a. EL DESAYUNO   **b.** el almuerzo

c. LA MERIENDA   **d.** LA CENA

e. LA COMIDA

1	2	3	4	5

PART B.

Look at the picture of the family at the table. Listen to the statements that will be read to you twice. Decide if they are **true or false**. Check the appropriate box.

	1	2	3	4	5	6	7	8	9	10
true										
false										

MEAL TAKING

CONVERSATION WITH A PARTNER

SPEAKING

PART A.

Interview your conversation partner to find out what food he/she prefers for each meal below. Record your partner's answers to the right.

Ask: ¿Qué prefieres comer para <u>el desayuno</u>?
Answer: Prefiero <u>pan</u>.

EL DESAYUNO   _____

EL ALMUERZO   _____

LA CENA   _____

LA MERIENDA   _____

PART B.

Find out which foods your partner likes and which he/she dislikes by asking, "**¿Te gusta**_____?" while referring to the items listed below. Check your partner's responses in the boxes below.

	Sí	No
1. la margarina		
2. el brécol		
3. las espinacas		
4. las fresas		
5. los pasteles		
6. las papas fritas		
7. los espárragos		
8. las hamburguesas		
9. el queso		
10. el helado		

Now ask your partner which item he likes best from the entire list. **¿Cuál prefieres más?**
Circle the food your partner has chosen on the list.

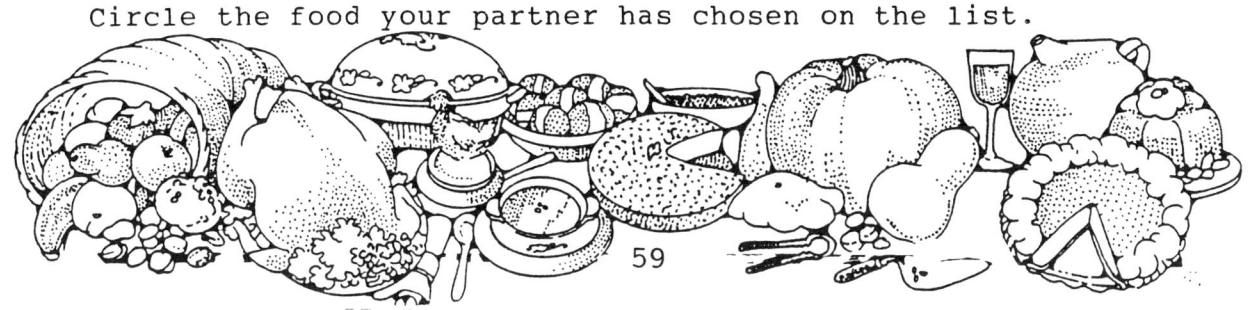

MEAL TAKING

PART C.

With your partner, use the following scrambled sentences and phrases to create a dialogue. Number the lines in a logical sequence.

_____ Muchas gracias.

_____ Aquí tiene el menú.

_____ Quisiera una mesa para <u>dos personas</u>.

_____ ¿Y algo de beber?

_____ ¿En qué puedo servirle?

_____ <u>No queremos el postre</u>. La cuenta, por favor.

_____ ¿Qué quieren comer?

_____ <u>Unos vinos blancos</u>.

_____ Dos platos de <u>langosta con papas y una ensalada</u>.

Now that you have unscrambled and practiced the dialogue above. Create your own dialogue between you and a waiter by replacing the underlined words.

PART D.

UNA ENTREVISTA

Interview your conversation partner to find out his/her preferences about food and meals.

1. ¿Cuál es tu comida favorita? _____

2. ¿Qué prefieres comer para el desayuno? _____

3. ¿A qué hora comes la merienda? _____

4. ¿Qué prefieres comer para la merienda? _____

5. ¿Dónde comes la cena? _____

6. ¿Quién prepara las comidas en tu familia? _____

7. ¿Cuándo comes la cena? _____

READING

PART A.

Read the menu for the new restaurant that has opened in your neighborhood, then answer the questions that follow in Spanish.

EL MESÓN PÉREZ

MENÚ TURÍSTICO - 1.000 pesetas

entremeses	ensaladas
ápio y aceitunas	de frutas mixtas
calamares fritos	de lechuga y tomate
coctel de camarones	de espinaca

PLATOS PRINCIPALES

el biftec con cebollas fritas	camarones fritos
chuletas de ternera	langosta con papas
paella valenciana	mariscada en salsa verde

*cada plato incluye pan y mantequilla y papas fritas

los vegetales del día

judías verdes, zanahorias o brécol

BEBIDAS

refrescos, jugo, vino, té, café

POSTRES

helado   flan   torta de piña   pastel de manzana

ABIERTO: lunes hasta viernes 18:00 - 22:00
sábado 16:00 - 22:00

---

1. What meal of the day is served in this restaurant?

_____

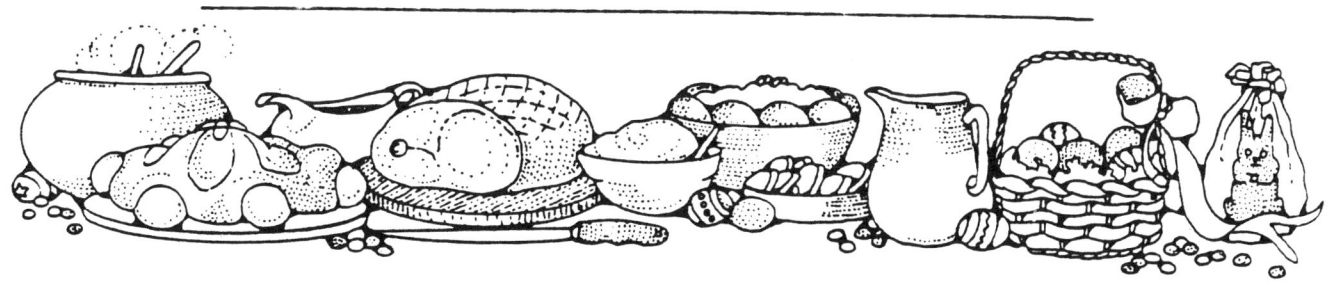

MEAL TAKING

2. What meals would a person who likes seafood order?

   a. _____ b. _____

   c. _____

3. If you don't like cake, what desserts can you order?

   a. _____ b. _____

4. What green vegetable can you order?

   _____

5. What is your favorite appetizer on this menu?

   _____

PART B.

Read the advertisement for the fruit store. There are many special prices for certain items. Answer the questions below by circling the correct response.

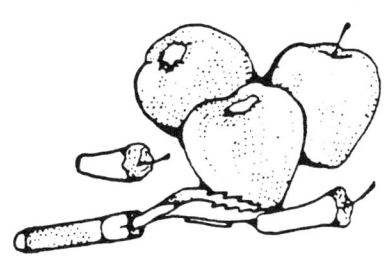

LA FRUTERÍA - LA MANZANA GRANDE

Una venta extraordinaria de frutas - el 6 y 7 de mayo

TENEMOS TODA CLASE DE FRUTAS A PRECIOS BAJOS

PERAS - 300 pesos por libra

MANZANAS - 500 pesos por libra

CEREZAS - 400 pesos por libra

UVAS - 250 pesos por libra

*También pida una ensalada de frutas mixtas por 650 pesos por libra

ESTA FRUTA ES LA MÁS FRESCA EN NUESTRO PUEBLO.

LLÁMENOS: 26-34-67

1. ¿Qué no se venden en esta tienda?

    a. frijoles   b. bananas   c. plátanos   d. uvas

2. ¿Cuánto cuestan dos libras de manzanas y tres libras de cerezas?

    a. 1.300   b. 2.200   c. 1.100   d. 1.800

3. Según el anuncio, ¿qué ofrece esta frutería?

    a. una sandía cortada   b. plátanos fritos
    c. ensalada de varias frutas d. batidos de frutas

PART C.

Read the advertisement for this restaurant in Perú and decide if the statements are **true or false**.

CAFÉ DEL MAR

UN RESTAURANTE
DESDE 1970

FAMOSO POR LA COMIDA DE PRIMERA CALIDAD

UN AMBIENTE AMABLE Y CÓMODO

ESPECIALIZANDO EN PLATOS DE PESCADO Y MARISCOS

PAELLA CON LANGOSTA ES NUESTRA ESPECIALIDAD

SE SIRVE LA COMIDA DE 1 - 3 P.M.
LA CENA DE 9 - 10 P.M.

Verdad o Mentira

1. _____ This restaurant was established about twenty years ago.

2. _____ Someone who likes to order steak would enjoy this restaurant.

3. _____ If you enjoy rice and seafood with saffron seasoning, you will be satisfied eating here.

4. _____ This restaurant serves "fast food".

5. _____ You will not be served between 3 and 8 p.m.

PART D.   MEAL TAKING

Read the store coupon and answer the questions below in Spanish.

 CUPÓN DEL FABRICANTE/ VÁLIDO HASTA 21/7/90

CAFÉ PURO DE COLOMBIA
RICO Y AROMÁTICO

AHORRE   60¢

REGULAR   DECAFEINADO

1. ¿Cuánto es el descuento? _____

2. ¿Cómo es este café? _____

3. ¿Qué dos clases de café hay? _____
   _____

4. ¿Cuál es el último día que puedes usar este cupón?
   _____

MAKE YOUR OWN COUPON IN SPANISH

1. Draw your product   2. Name it   3. Discount it.
4. Describe it in Spanish.

```
_____

_____
        Nombre del producto

_____
              Descuento

_____
        Descripción del producto

Dibuje el producto
```

MEAL TAKING

ESCRIBAMOS

WRITING

PART A.

List five food items for each category below in Spanish.

PAN Y CEREAL

1. _____
2. _____
3. _____
4. _____
5. _____

VEGETALES

1. _____
2. _____
3. _____
4. _____
5. _____

LA CARNE

1. _____
2. _____
3. _____
4. _____
5. _____

LA FRUTA

1. _____
2. _____
3. _____
4. _____
5. _____

WRITING IN SPANISH  MEAL TAKING

PART B.

You are planning a menu for a party you are having this weekend with your friends. Write a shopping list of ten items you need.

1_____ 2_____
3_____ 4_____
5_____ 6_____
7_____ 8_____
9_____ 10_____

PART C.

Your mother asks you to check the refrigerator for items she needs from the dairy. Help her by writing down 4 dairy items she needs.

1_____ 2_____
3_____ 4_____

 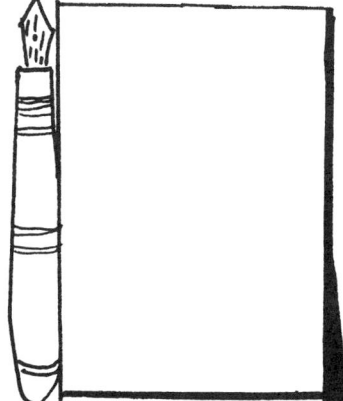

MEAL TAKING

PART D.

You have invited some friends for dinner tonight, but
realize that you forgot to buy some items you will need.
Leave a note telling your friends why you are not home.

SPEAKING SITUATIONS

MEAL TAKING

In pairs, prepare the conversations by playing the roles indicated in the situations.

You are in your favorite restaurant. Your friend from Spanish class is also waiting for a table. Greet him or her and mention why you like this restaurant.

You are very hungry. Convince your best friend to go to a Spanish restaurant for dinner.

You and your friend are planning a picnic this Saturday. Decide what each person is going to bring. Discuss other important details.

You are at dinner in a very fancy restaurant. Tell the waiter your order. Then mention one problem you are having with the food or service.

SOPA DE LETRAS   MEAL TAKING

Write the English for each word. Then find these words in the puzzle.

** LAS COMIDAS **

```
H D R P L A T O D D R U J Q P T S H P G
U T F P A U P A P A S V P D V O X M V O
V V W S E P S O P A T A A Z U C A R P J
L C A C S R R P Y C J A M O N Q Z F L B
Y F L Y G Y A R S L A T L H F X O H A O
D N M V M F R E S A S M A E E R V L T V
M J U C D T O R T A J W A Z C D S Y A Z
F U E A U P P E S C A D O R A H D B N E
M D R T L S U Y Z J X C A A E Q U S O A
Z I Z E C N A R A N J A X G O R P G R X
G A O L E V I N O L W R O U D Q O F A B
O S O L S V I M Q B C N R A O J O C X J
L V I I V K P P A O O E P Y M Z O R R A
I E O V Z Y R O L N N D B B I F T E C B
M R G R P S E L N J Z N A O F A X K D Q
O D Q E W O I L O P Y A X L L R L I T O
N E D S X H C O K A S R N U E L U H G C
O S R I C T M E R I E N D A V H A T R R
J H W U F O G X J D B R E A K F A S T X
A N C R M A N T E Q U I L L A S C X N W
```

TAZA_____   CEBOLLA_____

CUCHILLO_____   HELADO_____

VINO_____   BIFTEC_____

SOPA_____   LECHUGA_____

NARANJA_____   LIMÓN_____

DULCES_____   PLATO_____

PAPAS_____   FRESAS_____

CARNE_____   TORTA_____

JAMON_____   MERIENDA_____

JUDIAS VERDES_____   PLATANO_____

ALMUERZO_____   CAMARERO_____

SERVILLETA_____   MANZANA_____

ARROZ_____   POLLO_____

AGUA_____   MANTEQUILLA_____

PESCADO_____   AZUCAR_____

UVA_____   PERA_____

SHOPPING

AIMS

you will be able to...

- describe clothing.
- express prices in pesos and pesetas.
- read advertisements for various types of stores.
- fill out mail order catalogue forms.
- converse with a salesclerk.
- identify various stores and what each sells.

LISTENING

PART A.

Listen carefully to each description that will be read to you twice and write the number of the description next to the appropriate picture.

PART B.

You are in a clothing store in Cancún, México. The salesclerk asks you a few questions. Listen carefully to each question that will be read to you twice. Choose the best response and write the letter of that response in the space provided.

1._____   a. No, eso es todo, gracias.

2._____   b. Me gusta el color rojo.

3._____   c. Necesito talla pequeña.

4._____   d. No me gusta el color.

5._____   e. Pago con tarjeta de crédito.

     f. Quisiera una blusa.

SHOPPING

CONVERSATION WITH A PARTNER

SPEAKING

PART A.

You are going shopping today. First, tell your partner what you must buy. Then, after your partner has suggested a store, find out where the store is located. (Follow the model below)

Ejemplo:
1. Quiero comprar <u>aspirinas</u>.
2. Ve a <u>la farmacia</u>.
1. ¿Dónde está <u>la farmacia</u>?
2. Está al lado <u>del supermercado</u>.

ITEMS

- manzanas
- carne
- papas
- botas
- medicina
- churros
- langosta
- un diccionario
- un anillo de oro
- pantalones
- huevos

STORES

- la pastelería
- la ropería
- la librería
- la joyería
- la pescadería
- la zapatería
- la lechería
- la frutería
- la verdulería
- la farmacia
- la carnicería

PART B.

You are in a clothing store in Mexico City. One of you will play the role of a salesclerk and the other will be the customer. The salesclerk will find out what the customer wants to buy by asking the appropriate questions in order to fill out the receipt.

Ropería Galdós.

Insurgentes, 62
28065 México D.F.
Tel. 33.76.88

****

CANTIDAD	DESCRIPCIÓN	COLOR	PRECIO
		TOTAL (I.V.A. incluído)	

SHOPPING

PART C.

You go to the information desk at the CORTE FRANCÉS department store in Barcelona. One of you will play the role of a salesclerk and the other will be the customer. The customer will ask the salesclerk for assistance in finding out where certain items can be purchased.

Ejemplo: 1. ¿Dónde están <u>los libros</u>?
          2. Están en la <u>octava planta</u>

EL CORTE FRANCÉS

PLANTA		DEPARTAMENTO
9	☆	JUGUETERÍA
8	★	LIBRERÍA
7	☆	MUEBLES
6	★	ELECTRODOMÉSTICOS
5	☆	DEPORTES
4	★	ROPA PARA HOMBRES
3	☆	ROPA PARA NIÑOS
2	★	ROPA PARA SEÑORAS
1	☆	ZAPATERÍA

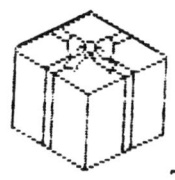

READING

PART A.

Read the following descriptions of items from a Spanish mail order catalogue. Then answer the questions in Spanish.

A Zapatos para señoras
Cuero.
Tallas: 36 - 40
36-699 tl pardo
36-167 ml negro
36-598 tm gris
.......6000 ptas

B Traje de baño
Dos piezas
Tallas: 40 - 48
27-700 dl rosado
27-568 ul amarillo
27-874 pl blanco
......2300 ptas

C Abrigo para señoras
Pura lana 100%
Tamaños: 44 - 54
18-854 ul rojo
18-796 sl negro
18-843 zl gris
......15000 ptas

D Pantalones para hombres
de poliéster
Tallas: 44 - 54
35-934 dl negro
35-938 rl verde oscuro
35-946 ll azul
.......3400 ptas

E Suéter de lana
Hecho a mano
Tallas: 40 - 50
17-789 sl violeta
17-788 zl verde
17-824 dl negro
......4500 ptas

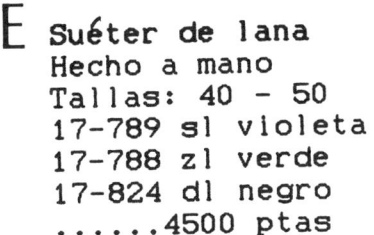

F Chaqueta para hombres
lana 60% - poliéster 40%
Tallas 46 - 56
diseño a cuadros
.......6000 ptas

*   *   *

1.¿Cuál es la cosa más cara?_____

2.¿Qué llevas en el invierno?_____

3.¿Qué llevas en el verano?_____

4.¿Cuáles son los colores de los zapatos para señoras?
_____

5.¿Qué llevas para ir a una fiesta elegante? _____

PART B.

Read these ads from a Spanish Yellow Pages. Then answer the questions in English.

RELOJERÍA LA HORA

ESPECIALIZADO EN REPARACIONES DE RELOJES ANTIGUOS, CUARZO, SUIZOS Y JAPONESES

Pl de España, 17

Tel 247 41 51

MADRID

---

zapatería Pepe

PARA HOMBRES, SEÑORAS Y NIÑOS

LAS MEJORES MARCAS DE BOLSAS, ZAPATOS Y CINTURONES

PLAZA MAYOR, 9
TEL. 763 54 21

TOLEDO

LIBRERÍA AZTECA

- La más amplia selección de libros para todos los colegios.

- Tenemos libros de arte, historia, geografía, ciencias, y literatura.

- También tenemos mapas, revistas y periódicos.

Avenida del Puerto, 9
Tel. 345 87 54

VALENCIA

FARMACIA CENTRAL

Grandes descuentos en recetas médicas

Servicio de 24 horas

Plaza Cataluña, 7
tel. 328 65 43

BARCELONA

---

1. In what city is the clock and watch store located? _____

2. What items are sold at the shoe store? _____

3. Where would you go if you needed to buy a map? _____

4. What is offered at the Farmacia Central? _____

5. Where would you go if you wanted to purchase a belt? _____

WRITING

PART A.

You are going on a summer vacation to Puerto Plata in the Dominican Republic. In Spanish, list four items you want to buy for your summer wardrobe.

_____

_____

_____

_____

PART B.

You will be going skiing in the Andes. List four items you will bring with you in Spanish.

_____

_____

_____

_____

PART C.

Your grandmother from Honduras sent a present for your birthday. Write a note, in Spanish, thanking her for the gift and explaining why you like it.

_____

_____

_____

_____

_____

CRUCIGRAMA   SHOPPING

ACROSS CLUES

1. jacket
3. suit
6. black
7. gloves
9. socks
15. pants
16. skirt
17. hat
19. sweater
21. red
22. scarf
24. pink
25. white

DOWN CLUES

1. tie
2. belt
4. green
5. grey
8. blouse
9. necklace
10. raincoat
11. watch (clock)
12. umbrella
13. dress
14. t-shirt
18. brown
20. yellow
23. blue

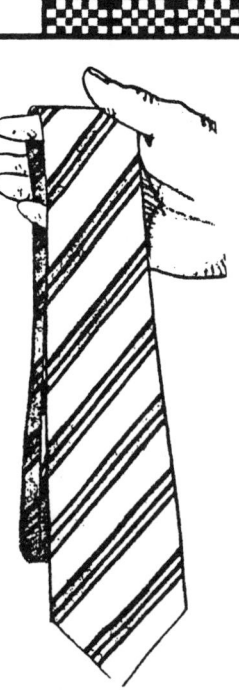

SHOPPING
SPEAKING SITUATIONS

In pairs, prepare the conversation playing the roles indicated in the situation.

You meet a friend in the mall. Discuss where both of you are going and what you will buy.

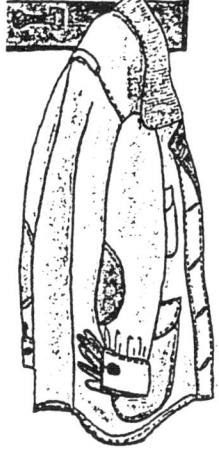

Convince your mother or father to give you money for an outfit you saw today at the store.

Your brother suggests a gift to buy for your cousin's birthday. Disagree, tell why, and suggest something else.

You are in a clothing store. Tell the salesperson what you need and purchase it.

HEALTH AND WELFARE

AIMS

You will be able to....

- name the parts of the body and their functions.
- make an appointment with the doctor.
- fill out a medical form.
- tell your symptoms to a doctor.
- identify illnesses and give appropriate remedies.

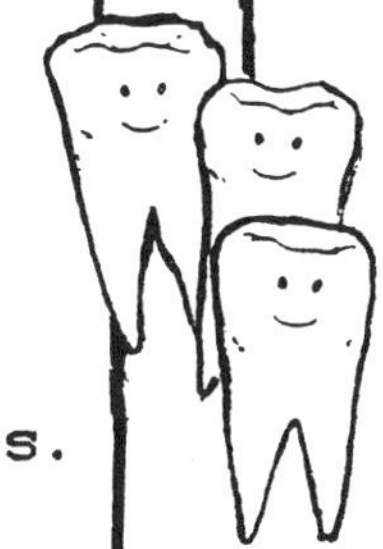

LISTENING

HEALTH AND WELFARE

PART A.

While you are at a party, some people are talking about what they do. Match what they say with the body part associated with that activity. Listen carefully to the statement that will be read twice to you, and write the number of the sentence next to the picture.

PART B.   HEALTH AND WELFARE

You are at the doctor's office in Puerto Rico. While there you overhear Dr. Mendoza describing his patients. Listen carefully to the descriptions that will be read twice to you. Write the name of the patient above the picture being described.

Gloria   Jorge   **María**   Tomás

Luis   **Elena**   Juan

HEALTH AND WELFARE

CONVERSATION WITH A PARTNER

SPEAKING

PART A.

While on vacation in Mexico, you become ill. You go to the doctor's office for treatment. Before you see the doctor, the nurse must fill out your vital information for the doctor's records. One of you will play the role of the nurse and fill out the form below. The other student will play the role of the patient and answer the questions.

Dr. Ricardo Más López
Insurgentes, 65
México D.F., México
Tel. 34-23-89

FORMULARIO DEL CONSULTORIO

FECHA_____

APELLIDO_____ NOMBRE_____

DIRECCIÓN_____CIUDAD_____

CÓDIGO POSTAL_____

TELÉFONO (   ) _____

EDAD_____ FECHA DE NACIMIENTO_____

OCUPACIÓN_____

ENFERMEDADES INFANTILES_____

COMPAÑÍA DE SEGUROS_____

SÍNTOMAS Y DIAGNOSIS_____
_____

FIRMA DEL PACIENTE_____

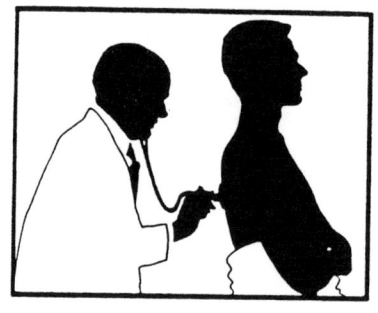

PART B.   HEALTH AND WELFARE

Your partner doesn't feel well. Find out **what** is wrong and give him/her two suggestions.

Ejemplo: 1. ¿Qué tienes?
          2. <u>Tengo un dolor de muelas</u>. ¿Qué debo hacer?
          1. <u>Ve al dentista</u> y no <u>comas mucho</u>.

un dolor de cabeza un dolor de muelas una tos un dolor de garganta una gripe un dolor de espalda una fiebre un dolor de estómago la pierna rota un resfriado	Ve al médico. No salgas. Toma dos aspirinas. Descansa. Ve a casa. Ve al dentista. No camines al colegio. Bebe mucho. No hables tanto. No comas.

READING

HEALTH AND WELFARE

PART A.

Luis Ortega's doctor has given him the following prescription. Read it and answer the questions in English.

Dra. María Maradona García

Florida, 55
993075 - Buenos Aires
(tel) 54-6776

PACIENTE: APELLIDO _Ortega_ NOMBRE _Luis_
DIRECCION _Calle Cervantes, 3, B.A._ EDAD _7_
SINTOMAS _Fiebre un poco alta_
INSTRUCCIONES _tome una píldora por la mañana y por la noche. Beba muchos líquidos y guarde cama de la 3 días_

---

1. How old is Luis? _____

2. What symptoms does Luis have? _____

3. What type of medicine must Luis take? _____

4. In addition to taking medicine, what other recommendations has the doctor given on the prescription?

_____

HEALTH AND WELFARE

PART B.

Read this article from a Mexican science fiction magazine. Then draw what is being described.

MÉXICO. Según los habitantes del pequeño pueblo de Extrañadura en la región noroeste del país, ha llegado una nave espacial con un grupo de extraterrestres del planeta Equis. "Son muy raros," dijo Juan Manuel Obregón, " y son muy bajos. Tienen tres cabezas. En cada cabeza tienen tres ojos grandes, dos bocas pequeñas y cuatro narices. No tienen pelo, son calvos. Sus brazos son muy largos y tienen seis dedos en cada mano. Tienen las piernas muy cortas y los pies muy grandes." Juan Manuel también nos dijo que salieron tan pronto como llegaron. ¡Qué lástima que no tuviéramos la oportunidad de conocerlos mejor!

HEALTH AND WELFARE

WRITING

PART A.

You are going shopping. In Spanish, list five health or grooming products you will buy there.

PART B.

You have the flu. Write a list of four symptoms that you have in Spanish

PART C.

You are sick. Leave a note, in Spanish, telling your friend why you cannot meet him/her after school today.

HEALTH AND WELFARE
SOPA DE LETRAS

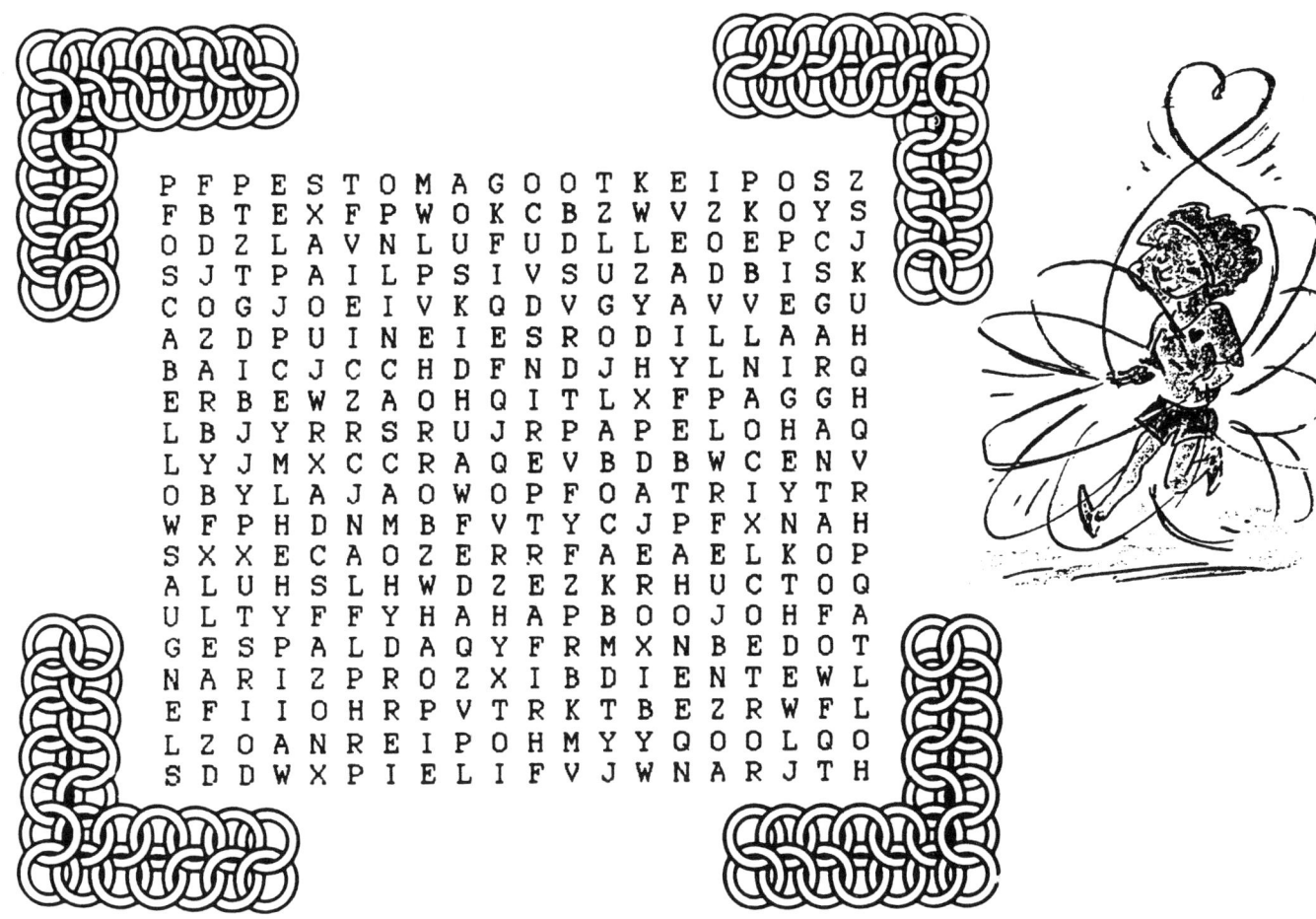

```
P F P E S T O M A G O O T K E I P O S Z
F B T E X F P W O K C B Z W V Z K O Y S
O D Z L A V N L U F U D L L E O E P C J
S J T P A I L P S I V S U Z A D B I S K
C O G J O E I V K Q D V G Y A V V E G U
A Z D P U I N E I E S R O D I L L A A H
B A I C J C C H D F N D J H Y L N I R Q
E R B E W Z A O H Q I T L X F P A G G H
L B J Y R R S R U J R P A P E L O H A Q
L Y J M X C C R A Q E V B D B W C E N V
O B Y L A J A O W O P F O A T R I Y T R
W F P H D N M B F V T Y C J P F X N A H
S X X E C A O Z E R R F A E A E L K O P
A L U H S L H W D Z E Z K R H U C T O Q
U L T Y F F Y H A H A P B O O J O H F A
G E S P A L D A Q Y F R M X N B E D O T L
N A R I Z P R O Z X I B D I E N T E W L
E F I I O H R P V T R K T B E Z R W F L
L Z O A N R E I P O H M Y Y Q O O L Q O
S D D W X P I E L I F V J W N A R J T H
```

LIST OF WORDS

CABEZA	PELO	OJO
BOCA	LENGUA	GARGANTA
ESPALDA	BRAZO	DEDO
ESTOMAGO	RODILLA	PIEL
HOMBRO	CARA	CABELLO
OREJA	DIENTE	NARIZ
CUELLO	MANO	PECHO
PIERNA	PIE	

------------ ------------ ------------ ------------ ------------
------------ ------------ ------------ ------------ ------------
------------ ------------ ------------ ------------ ------------
------------ ------------ ------------ ------------ ------------
------------ ------------

HEALTH AND WELFARE
SPEAKING SITUATIONS

In pairs, prepare the conversation playing the roles indicated in the situation.

You call up a friend to make plans for the day but he/she isn't feeling well. Discuss his/her illness. Then make plans for another day.

You are on vacation in Venezuela. You go to a pharmacy because you are feeling ill. Tell the pharmacist what is wrong and ask for his/her advice.

You don't feel well. Tell your parent what is wrong and convince him/her to let you stay home from school.

You have just had a medical examination. The doctor gives you his diagnosis and suggests some remedies. React to his suggestions.

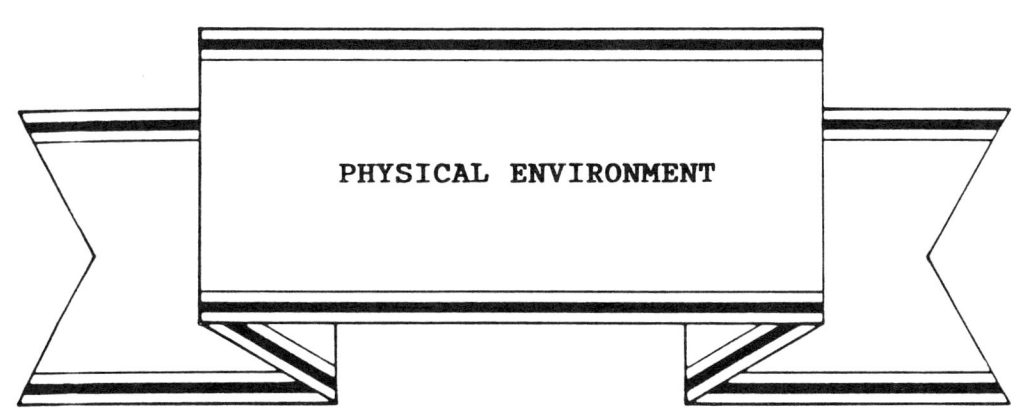

PHYSICAL ENVIRONMENT

You will be able to...

- identify seasons, climate, and weather conditions.

- identify basic geographical features.

- identify common animals.

- express your vacation preferences.

- read a weather report, a map, and environmental information.

- discuss activities appropriate to various places and weather conditions.

PHYSICAL ENVIRONMENT

LISTENING

PART A.

You are listening to your short wave radio and you hear weather conditions from around the world. Match the conditions in each weather report with the correct picture below. Write the letter of the correct answer in the appropriate box. Each weather report will be read twice.

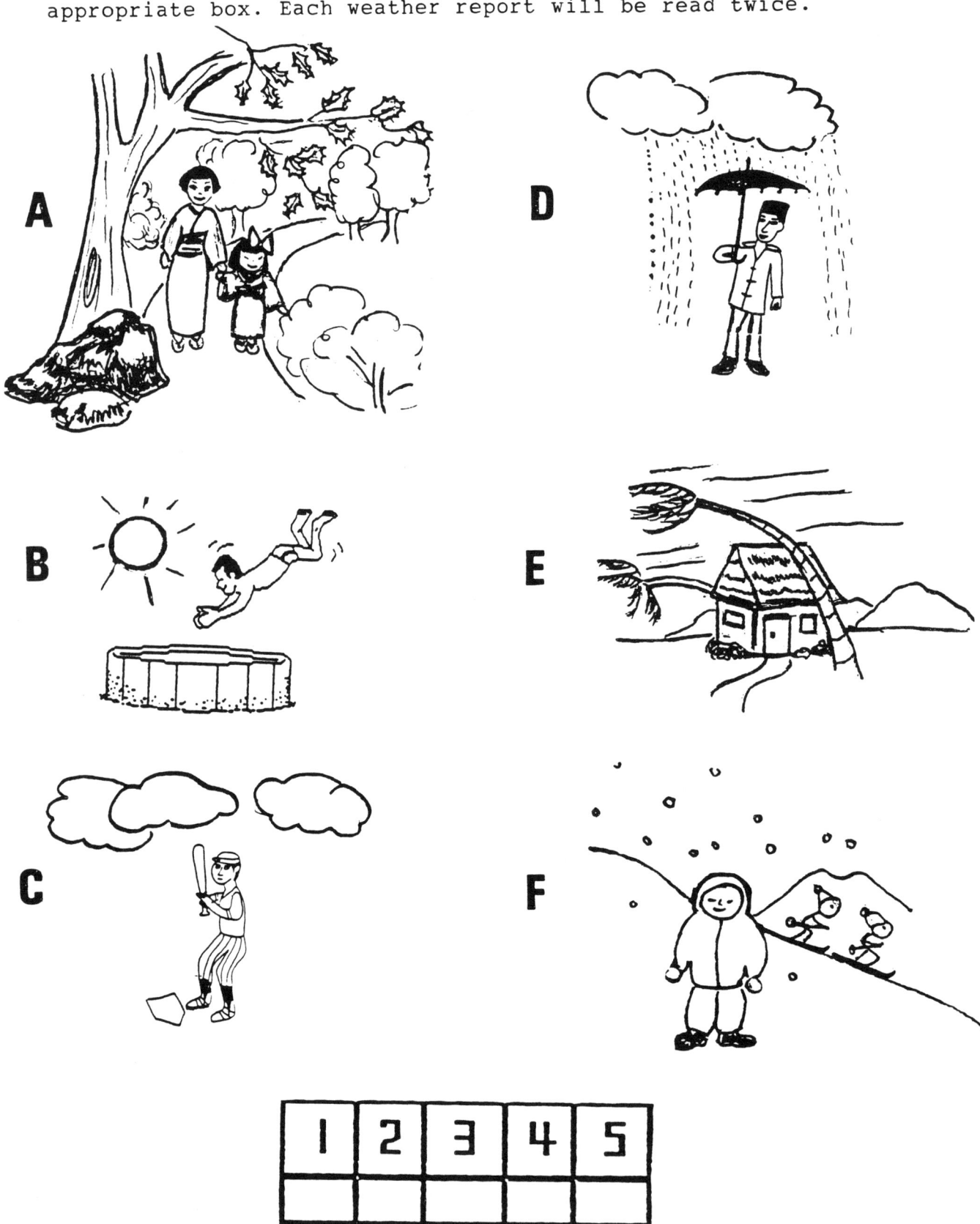

LISTENING   PHYSICAL ENVIRONMENT

PART B.

You are at a large reception and are listening to five people tell where they live. Match what the person says with the correct picture. Write the letter of your answer in the appropriate box. Each statement will be read twice.

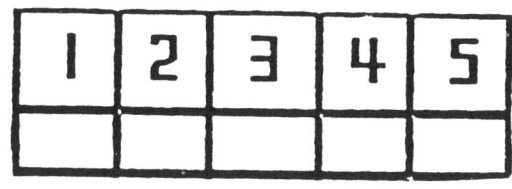

PHYSICAL ENVIRONMENT

SPEAKING

CONVERSATION WITH A PARTNER

PART A.

You are working in the Information Center at a national park. Your partner is playing the role of a park visitor. Give him/her directions to the various places on the map that he/she requests.

Sugerencias: Vaya ...   Camine..... Pase.....
              Pare....   Siga....... Doble....
              Cruce....   Suba....... Mire.....

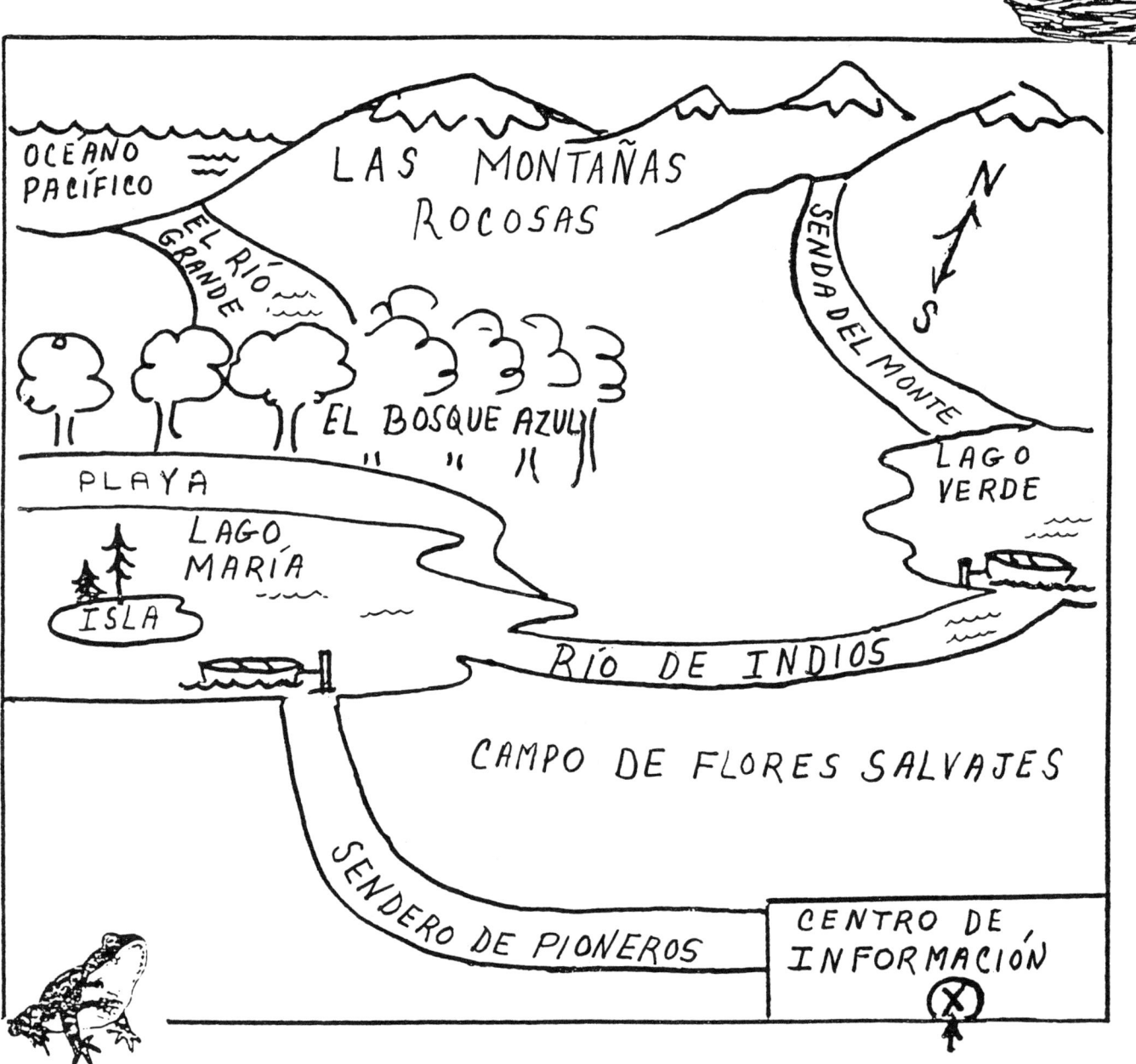

PHYSICAL ENVIRONMENT

SPEAKING

PART B.

UNA ENTREVISTA

You are a counselor at a camp. Interview your partner and find out his/her preferences regarding activities done outdoors. Fill out the following form by asking questions.

NOMBRE DE COMPAÑERO DE CONVERSACIÓN _____

Pregúntale: Te gusta .....mucho?

ACTIVIDAD	MUCHO	POCO	NADA
CORRER	X		
ESQUIAR			
ESQUIAR ACUÁTICO			
ACAMPAR			
ESCALAR MONTAÑAS			
VIAJAR			
VER PELÍCULAS			
NADAR			
TOMAR EL SOL			
PESCAR			
PATINAR			
IR DE COMPRAS			
JUGAR A LOS DEPORTES			

PHYSICAL ENVIRONMENT

READING

PART A.

TODOS SE DIVIERTEN EN EL ANIVERSARIO DEL ZOOLOGICO DE CHAPULTEPEC

Ayer fue un día de fiesta especial en el parque zoológico de Chapultepec. Más de mil niños de entre siete y doce años comieron un enorme pastel, palomitas y helados para celebrar el 67 aniversario del parque. En grupos, los niños oyeron la explicación de los hábitos de los animales que ahí se encuentran. El que más les llamó la atención fue el "bebé" hipopótamo que nadó con su madre. La directora del zoológico, Marielena Hoyo les informó que al parecer el recién nacido oso Panda y su madre Tohui se encuentran en perfectas condiciones.
Hay 280 diferentes especies de animales incluyendo: tigres, leones, elefantes, coyotes, culebras, pájaros, monos y osos.
El oso Panda es la única panda de segunda generación nacida fuera de la China.

Read the article and answer the questions below in Spanish.

1. ¿Qué se celebra en el Parque Zoólogico de Chapultepec?
   _____

2. ¿Quiénes participan?
   _____

3. ¿Qué hacen?
   _____

4. ¿Cuántas clases de animales hay en este zoólogico?
   _____

5. ¿Cuál animal es el que más les interesa a todos los visitantes?
   _____

PART B.   PHYSICAL ENVIRONMENT

You are planning to vacation at a national park this year. Read the advertisement for Ordesa National Park to help you decide if it has the activities you want. **Answer the questions on the next page.**

EL PARQUE NACIONAL DE ORDESA
EN EL PIRINEO ARAGONÉS

¿QUÉ OFRECE EL PARQUE AL TURISTA?

EN OTOÑO:
HAY LAS EXCURSIONES A PIE. MUCHAS VECES SE ULTILIZAN LOS VEHÍCULOS TODO TERRENO PARA IR MÁS RÁPIDAMENTE.
LOS MÁS AVENTUREROS TIENEN LA OPORTUNIDAD DE HACER EL DESCENSO DE CAÑONES
(UN NUEVO DEPORTE QUE ES UNA MEXCLA DE MONTAÑISMO Y NATACIÓN) Y NADAR EN LAS AGUAS EN LAS CUEVAS.

EN INVIERNO:
HAY TODA CLASE DE ESQUÍ: EL ESQUÍ FUERA DE PISTAS, EL ESQUÍ TRAVESÍA Y, COMO NOVEDAD, LAS EXCURSIONES CON RAQUETAS DE NIEVE.

EN VERANO:
HAY DIVERTIDAS RUTAS CON BICICLETA DE MONTAÑA, LAS MARCHAS ECUESTRES, EL PIRAGÜISMO (CANOEING) Y EL PARAPENTE (HANG-GLIDING).

VIAJES ORGANIZADOS

PARA DISFRUTAR DE LAS AVENTURAS SIN RIESGOS INNECESARIOS LOS TURISTAS PUEDEN PARTICIPAR EN VARIOS VIAJES ORGANIZADOS

EQUIPAJE:

EN CADA VIAJE PROGRAMADO, EN GENERAL, HAY QUE LLEVAR: UNAS BOTAS DE TREKKING, MOCHILA, SACO DE DORMIR, CHUBASQUERO (RAIN GEAR), UN ABRIGO, GORRO, GAFAS DE SOL Y ROPA APROPRIADA.

PARA MÁS INFORMACIÓN LLAME

PIRINEOS SIN FRONTERAS
TELÉFONO (975) 55 13 84

PHYSICAL ENVIRONMENT

Answer the following questions buy writing **Verdad** o **Mentira**.

_____ 1. Este parque está en España.

_____ 2. No hay programas organizados en el parque.

_____ 3. Cuando uno participa en deportes en el parque, debe llevar ropa similar a la de acampar.

_____ 4. Si prefiere ver películas y leer libros en casa, no va a divertirse mucho en el parque.

_____ 5. No puede montar bicicletas en el parque.

_____ 6. Estas actividades son para personas de buena salud.

_____ 7. El descenso de cañones es un nuevo deporte.

Now, write a list in Spanish of six activities you can do at the National Park of Ordesa.

_____   _____

_____   _____

_____   _____

READING

PART C.

PHYSICAL ENVIRONMENT

While traveling in Mexico you read this weather report to decide how to plan the rest of your trip.

PRONÓSTICO METEOROLÓGICO

Tiempo Nacional

ESTADO DEL TIEMPO

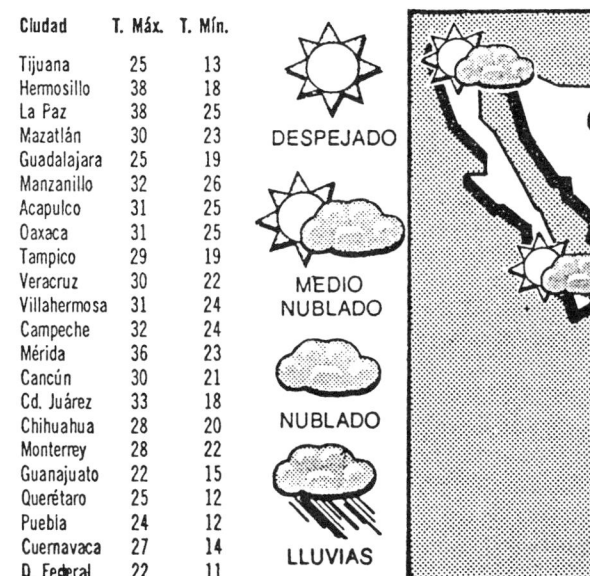

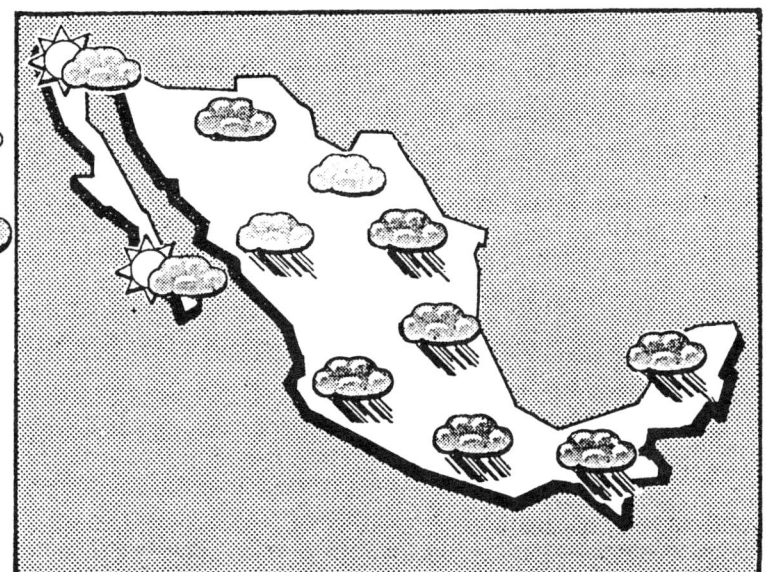

Ciudad	T. Máx.	T. Mín.
Tijuana	25	13
Hermosillo	38	18
La Paz	38	25
Mazatlán	30	23
Guadalajara	25	19
Manzanillo	32	26
Acapulco	31	25
Oaxaca	31	25
Tampico	29	19
Veracruz	30	22
Villahermosa	31	24
Campeche	32	24
Mérida	36	23
Cancún	30	21
Cd. Juárez	33	18
Chihuahua	28	20
Monterrey	28	22
Guanajuato	22	15
Querétaro	25	12
Puebla	24	12
Cuernavaca	27	14
D. Federal	22	11

DESPEJADO
MEDIO NUBLADO
NUBLADO
LLUVIAS

El pronóstico del tiempo para las próximas 24 horas indica que la tormenta tropical "Genevieve", estará al sur de San José del Cabo y la depresión tropical "Fausto" no es tan intensa.

Estará caluroso y nublado con lluvias en la mayor parte del territorio nacional, excepto en la península de Baja California, en donde estará medio nublado a despejado. (clearing)

La temperatura máxima registrada ayer fue de 39 grados centígrados en Altar, Sonora y la mínima de 10 grados en Zacatecas.

Answer the following questions in Spanish based on the report you just read.

1. What should you wear when you go out today?_____

2. How is the sky? _____

3. According to the map, what is the weather for southern Mexico? _____

PHYSICAL ENVIRONMENT

4. What is the forecast for the next twenty four hours?

   _____

5. What city had the highest temperature yesterday?

   _____

PART D.

Mexico City suffers from severe pollution because of its geographic location. Read the following chart and its key to answer the questions below.

Indice de Medición de Contaminacion Ambiental

EN LA CIUDAD DE MÉXICO, D.F.

Zona Noroeste: Contaminantes: 204 Ozono;
               79 Monóxido de Carbono.
Zona Centro: Contaminantes: 66 Ozono;
               387 Monóxido de Carbono.
Zona Sureste: Contaminantes: 127 Ozono;
               168 Monóxido de Carbono.

   0-100 Satisfactorio
   101-200 No Satisfactorio
   201-300 Malo
   301-500 Muy Malo

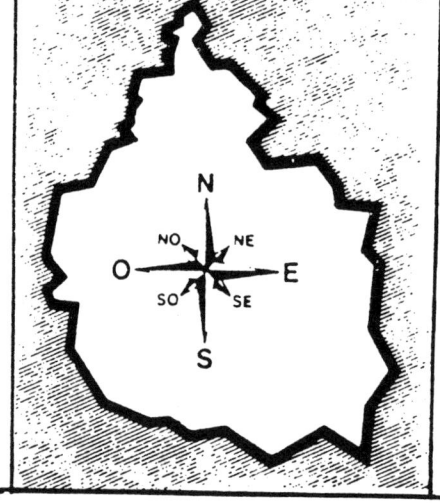

Circle the correct answers.

1. Which area has the worst problem with carbon monoxide?

   (Northeast, Central, Southeast)

2. Which area is classified as "Malo" for the ozone pollution?

   (Northeast, Central, Southeast)

3. Which zone is classified as "Satisfactorio" for carbon monoxide?

   (Northeast, Central, Southeast)

4. Which is the best zone in which to live?

   (Northeast, Central, Southeast)

PHYSICAL ENVIRONMENT

WRITING IN SPANISH

PART A.

Your family is going to buy a pet. Help your family decide on the right pet by listing five animals that can be pets.

PART B.

You and your friends are making plans for the weekend. Write a list of five activities you can do in or around town during the weekend.

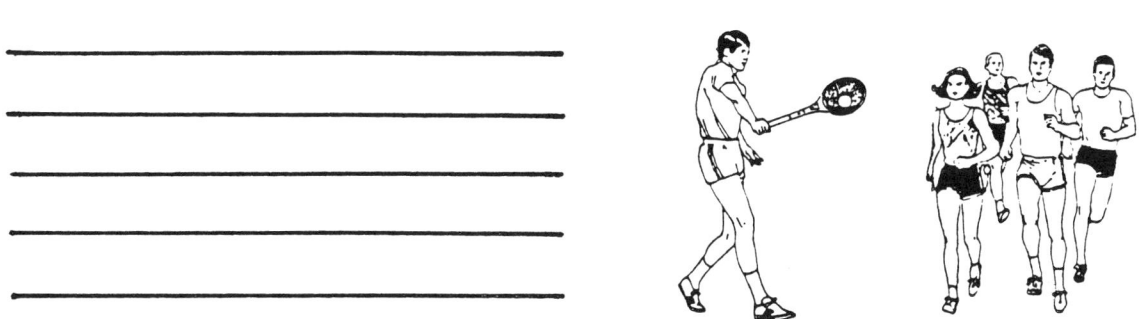

PART C.

Write a note inviting a friend to your summer house at the seashore. Tell him/her about the weather and at least five activities you can do together at the shore.

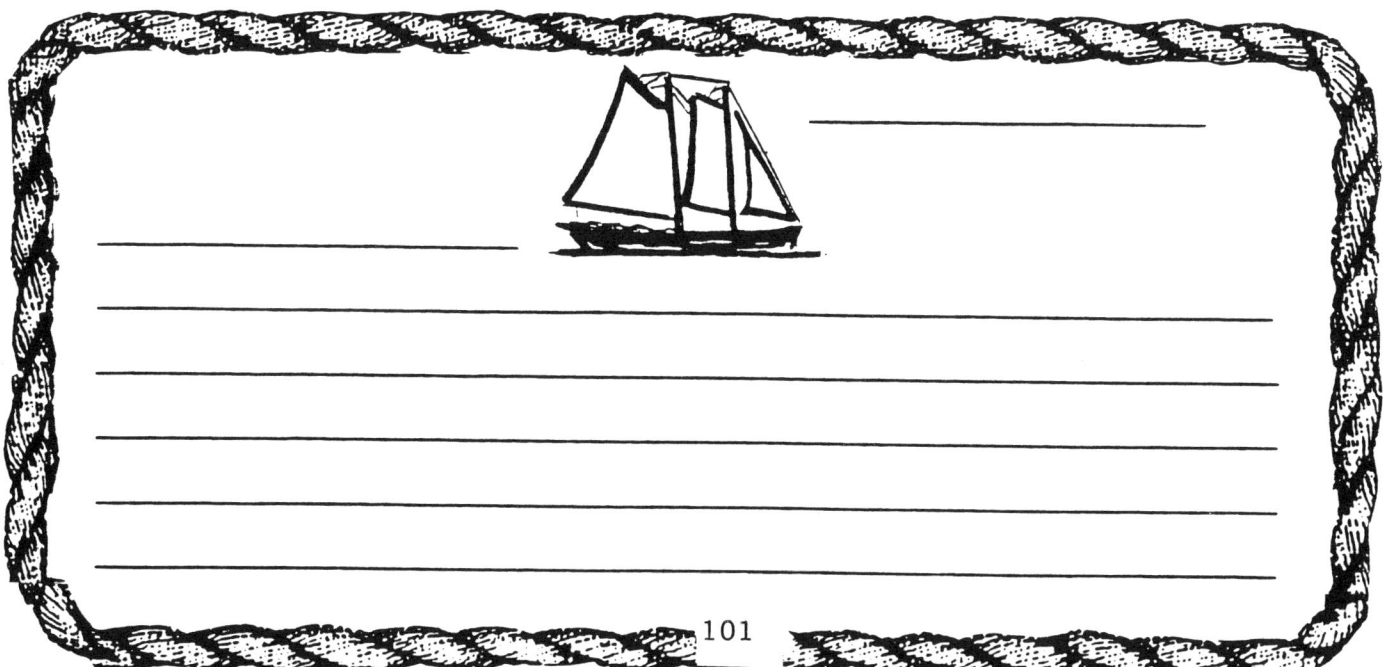

PHYSICAL ENVIRONMENT

EL MAPA

Your friend sent you a letter inviting you to visit him and
his family at their summer home near lake Titicaca in Perú.
From the information he has given you, draw a map of the area.

Hay un bosque pequeño al norte del lago Titicaca.
Juliaca es un pueblo pequeño cerca del lago, al oeste.
Muy lejos al este está el pueblo de Tipillas.
Al sur del lago se encuentra la hacienda de la familia Calancha.
Al este del lago está situada mi casa.

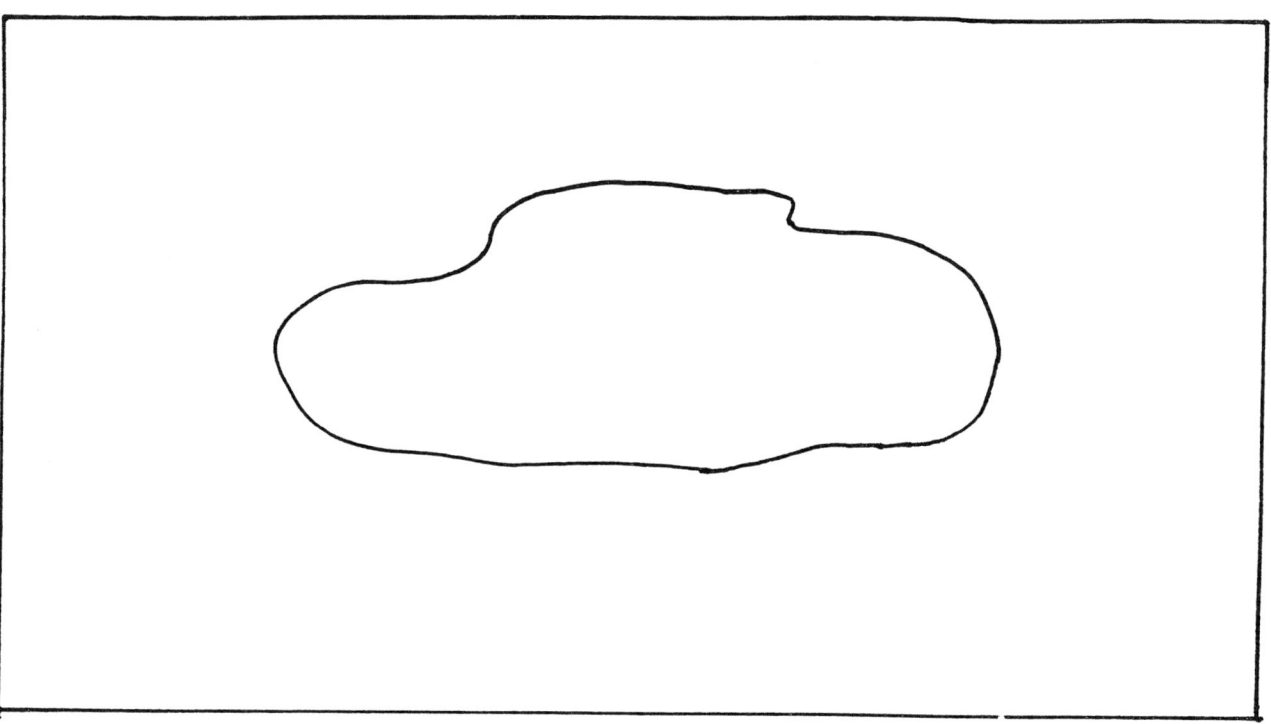

Now, on the above map, draw the path that he tells you to
take to his house:

Las instrucciones:
        Toma el tren para Tipillas para ir a Juliaca.
        Baja del tren en Juliaca.
        Camina a la hacienda de los Calanchas.
        Mi amigo, Rogelio Calancha, va a darte su bicicleta.
        Sigue al noreste para llegar a mi casa.

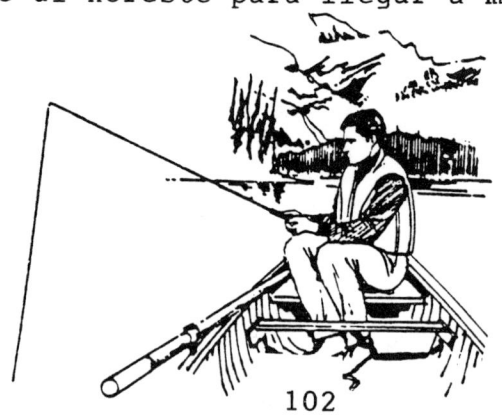

PHYSICAL ENVIRONMENT

ACROSS CLUES

1. farm
7. cows, for example
8. to play
11. city
12. river
14. to surf
15. countryside
18. to see
19. summer
20. neighbor
22. lake
23. forest
24. north
26. neighborhood
33. desert
34. spring
35. near
36. east

DOWN CLUES

2. to camp
3. sea
4. to fish
5. neighborhood
6. traffic
9. south
10. skyscraper
13. to swim
16. mountain
17. tree
21. island
25. to ski
27. building
28. fall, autumn
29. to run
30. the beach
31. west
32. far

SPEAKING SITUATIONS

PHYSICAL ENVIRONMENT

In pairs, prepare the conversations by playing roles indicated in the situations.

It is December school vacation. Convince your family to take a winter vacation.

The weather is bad. Your friend wants to go camping. React unfavorably and suggest going camping in better weather.

You are working in your state's tourist information bureau. Explain to a Spanish-speaking tourist your state's activities for various seasons.

You have been asked to go to the train station to pick up your friend's uncle who is coming from a farm in Peru. Greet him and converse about the climate, his farm, and the area in which he lives.

EARNING A LIVING

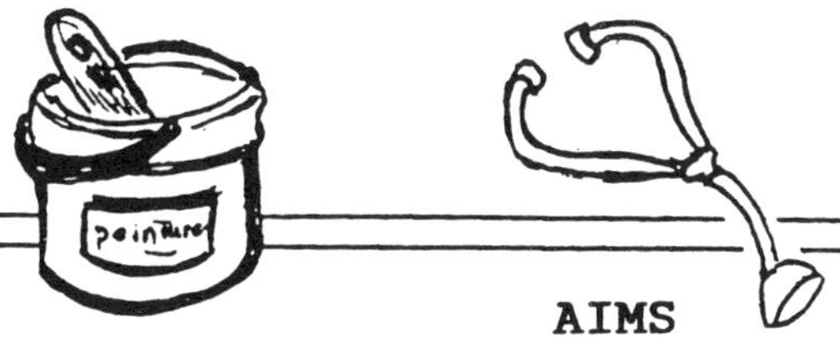

AIMS

You will be able to...

- identify different occupations.
- describe what people do and where they work.
- participate in a job interview.
- discuss the occupations in your family.
- express your feelings about different careers.
- read and understand help-wanted ads.

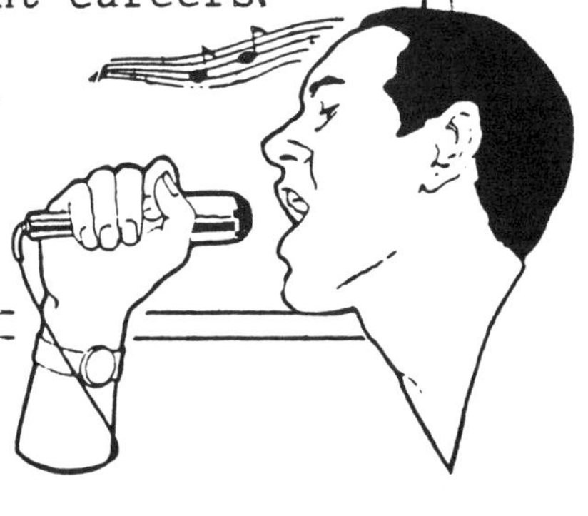

EARNING A LIVING

LISTENING

PART A.

Listen carefully to the job descriptions that will be read twice to you. Each one describes what a person does at work. Write the letter of the picture that illustrates the occupation described in the appropriate box.

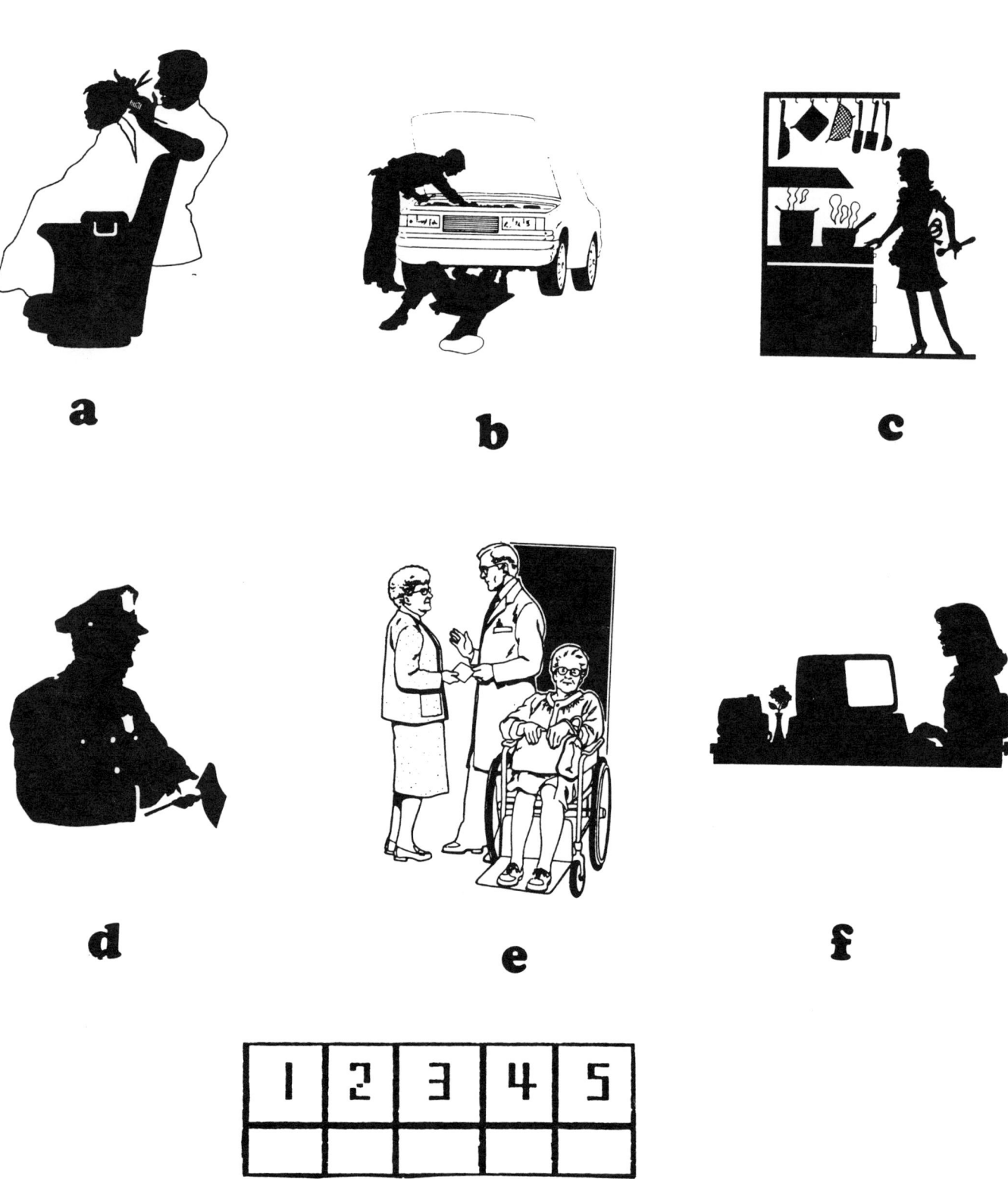

EARNING A LIVING

PART B.

Pedro is at a job interview. Listen carefully to the interview questions that will be read to you. Can you help him choose the best answers? Write the letter of your choice in the appropriate box.

A. Sí, yo hablo inglés y español.
B. Sí, hace seis años que yo tabajo en una compañía.
C. Sí, tengo un diploma.
D. Por supuesto, también soy programador.
E. Prefiero ser secretario.

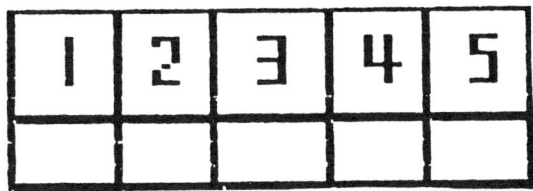

PART C.

Listen to these statements about various occupations that will be read to you. Decide if they are **true** or **false**. Then check the appropriate box.

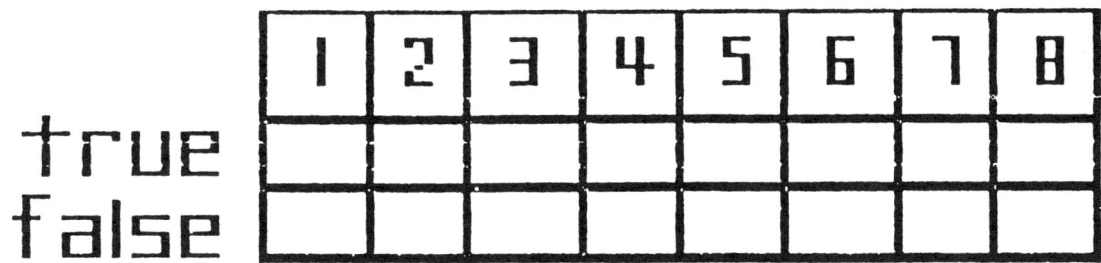

SPEAKING   EARNING A LIVING

CONVERSATION WITH A PARTNER

PART A.

La Familia y las Profesiones: Find out information about five members of your partner's family:
Ask: what they do and where they work.

You may include: uncles, aunts, cousins, etc.

Complete the form below based on your partner's answers.

Example: ¿Qué hace tu mamá? (papá)
¿Dónde trabaja ella? (él)

miembro de la familia	ocupación	lugar de empleo

PART B.

Ask your partner how he feels about different occupations. First make a list of five occupations. Then, ask your partner's opinion of each one. Record your partner's answers.

Ejemplo: 1. ¿Quiere ser bombero?
2. No.
1. ¿Por qué?
2. Es muy peligroso.

OCUPACIÓN	SÍ	NO	LA RAZÓN

EARNING A LIVING

PART C.

UNA ENCUESTA

Survey eight classmates to find out what they want to be.

Ask: ¿Qué quieres ser?   Answer: Yo quiero ser......

nombre del compañero de clase	ocupación

PART D.

DRAW AND GUESS WHO!

Draw a product, tool, or uniform of a particular occupation in each box. Then, ask your partner, "¿Para quién es ésto?" Your partner will tell who uses the item.
    Ejemplo: 1. ¿Para quién es ésto?
                   2. Es para un médico.

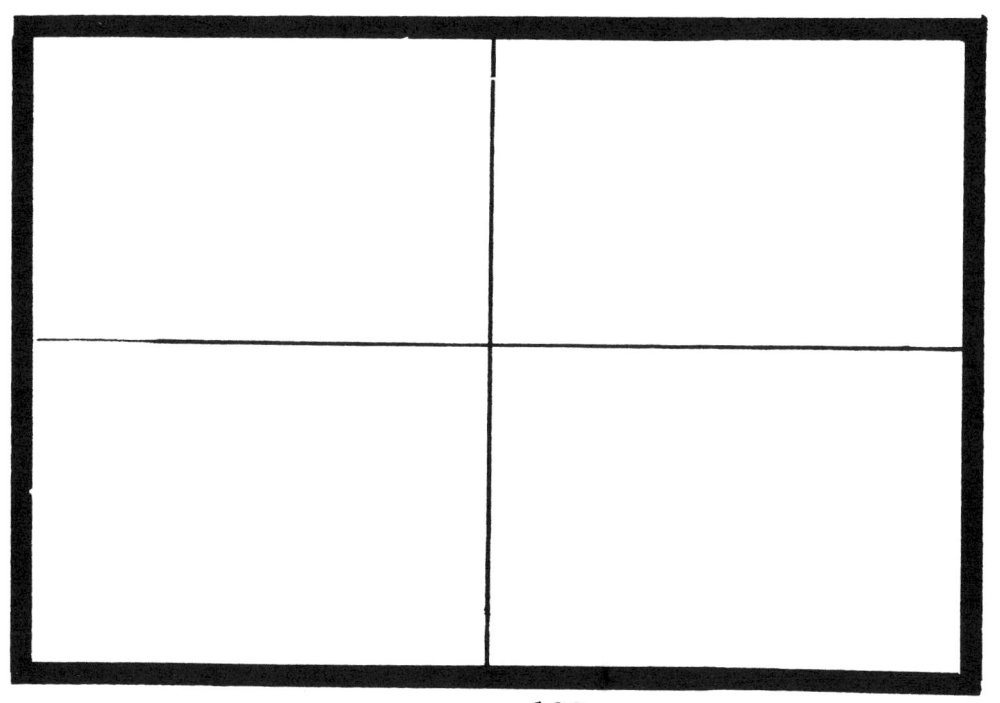

EARNING A LIVING

READING:

PART A.
You are considering moving to Buenos Aires and are reading the classified section of a newspaper to determine whether you are interested in any of the positions.

After reading each of these help-wanted ads, choose the correct answer to each question and write the letter in the space provided.

anuncios clasificados

EMPLEOS

a) MECÁNICOS

para mantenimiento
de sus vehículos
dos años de experiencia

Presentarse lunes y martes

de 9 a 15 hs.

EN AV. SARMIENTO 4045

b) ANALISTA PROGRAMADOR

Con experiencia
en sistemas interactivos
y base de datos, con
conocimiento de
administración de seguros
Antecedentes a Sr. Gerente

Av. Díaz Vélez 3873, 6º Piso
/Buenos Aires/

c) IMPORTANTE INSTITUCIÓN ASISTENCIAL DE CAPITAL FEDERAL NECESITA

SUPERVISOR DE FARMACIA

Debe poseer nivel
de instrucción secundaria,
experiencia en el puesto
Se ofrece: ingreso inmediato,
beneficios sociales
Debe hablar inglés y francés
Envie datos personales a:

VIAMONTE 1223

CAP. FED.

d) EMPRESA CONSTRUCTORA
Solicita

ARQUITECTO PARA OBRA EN EL SUR DEL PAÍS

Con experiencia en movimiento
de suelos y estructura.

Se ofrece: vivienda y
remuneración acorde a la
función.
Dirigirse por carta a:

CASILLA Correo 7153
Correo Central (1000)

Answer the questions according to the want ads.

1. For which job would you need to know several languages?
2. Which job requires knowledge of computers?
3. Which job requires two years of experience?
4. Which listing asks for higher education and experience?
5. Which position provides a place to live?
6. Which job requires a knowledge of automotives?

EARNING A LIVING

PART B. Read this employment ad. Then answer the questions in Spanish in the space provided.

Ingeniero Industrial

(ambos sexos)

Titular de un diploma universitario de Ingeniería Industrial y poseedor de una experiencia profesional de aproximadamente quince años.

Los candidatos deberán tener entre 35 y 40 años.

Los candidatos deberán tener experiencia en la construcción y explotación de sistemas de producción en la automación, robotización y control electrónico.

Deberán conocer bien el francés, y el inglés. Se apreciará el buen conocimiento de una tercera lengua comunitaria.

El EBI ofrece excelentes condiciones de empleo, una remuneración interesante (según aptitudes y experiencia) y numerosas ventajas de tipo social.

Envíe sus datos personales a la siguiente dirección:

BANCO ESPAÑOL DE INVERSIONES
Avenida del Sol 34
Madrid

Answer these questions in Spanish.

1. ¿Para quiénes es este puesto?
   _____

2. ¿Cuántos años de experiencia son necesarios?
   _____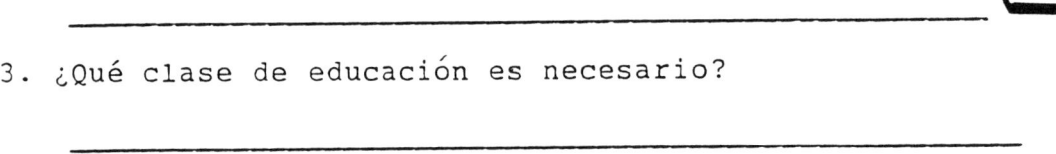

3. ¿Qué clase de educación es necesario?
   _____

4. ¿Cuántas lenguas deberá hablar un candidato?
   _____

5. ¿Cuántos años deberá tener un candidato?
   _____

6. ¿Por qué es un empleo interesante?_____

EARNING A LIVING

WRITING IN SPANISH

PART A.

You are at an employment agency. You tell the agent that you want a job for which you wear a uniform. Write a list of five occupations that you would consider.

_____

_____

_____

_____

_____

PART B.

You are applying for a job at a large company. On the application you are required to list five of your good qualities. Write them below in Spanish.

_____

_____

_____

_____

_____

EARNING A LIVING

PART C.

You have just started a new job in Argentina.. Write a note to your mother describing your work, what you do, and how you feel about it.

114

EARNING A LIVING

CREATE YOUR OWN HELP WANTED AD

Imagine that you are the personnel director of a company or a store. Write an advertisement for a job in your company. You may include the position, qualities desired, education, languages needed, experience, salary, reference requirements, name of company, address and telephone number.

clasificados

CREATE A BUSINESS CARD FOR YOUR IDEAL PROFESSION

You may include: your name, your ideal profession, your address, phone number, a logo or picture, a slogan about your work, and office hours.

EARNING A LIVING

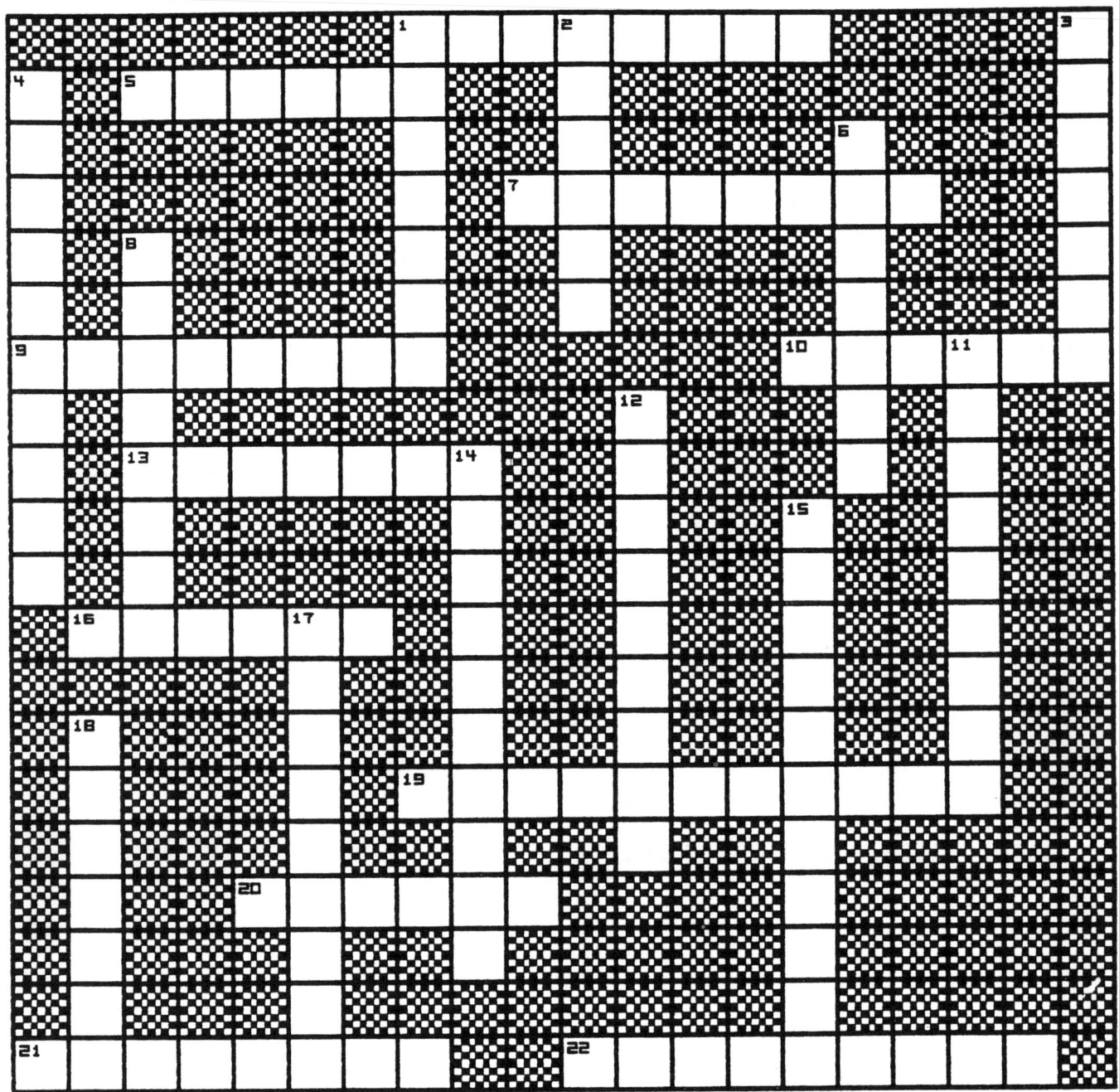

ACROSS CLUES

1. A man who fixes cars.
5. A person who models clothing.
7. A male teacher.
9. A person who fixes teeth.
10. A man who treats sick people.
13. Pablo Picasso is one.
16. A maid.
19. An animal doctor.
20. An athlete.
21. A woman who serves food in a restaurant.
22. A male nurse.

DOWN CLUES

1. A seamstress.
2. Elizabeth Taylor.
3. A man in the legal profession.
4. Someone who writes for a newspaper.
6. A man who puts out fires.
8. A man good with figures.
11. An engineer.
12. A man who styles your hair.
14. A woman who designs buildings.
15. A man who programs computers.
17. A person who investigates murders
18. An officer of the law.

SPEAKING SITUATIONS

EARNING A LIVING

In pairs, prepare the conversations by playing the roles indicated in the situations.

You are at a job interview speaking with the head of the company. Discuss your background and qualifications.

You and your guidance counselor are discussing your future. The guidance counselor wants to know what you want to do after finishing school.

You and a friend are discussing your career plans. Try to convince your friend to take the same type of job as you.

You and a friend are discussing the occupations of your parents or relatives. Say how you feel about what they do.

LEISURE

AIMS

You will be able to...

- identify and name types of T.V. programs, sports events and types of movies.

- talk about your favorite leisure activities.

- discuss T.V. programs you like to watch.

- read ads for concerts and T.V. shows.

- write a thank you note.

LEISURE

LISTENING

PART A.

You are listening to the radio and hear an announcement about tonight's T.V. programs. Write the number of the statement next to the corresponding T.V. program.
Each statement will be read twice.

	un anuncio
	un programa deportivo
	UN PRONÓSTICO
	LAS NOTICIAS
	un documentario

PART B.

You are at a party and your friends are giving their opinions about certain sports. Write the number of the statement you hear next to the appropriate picture.

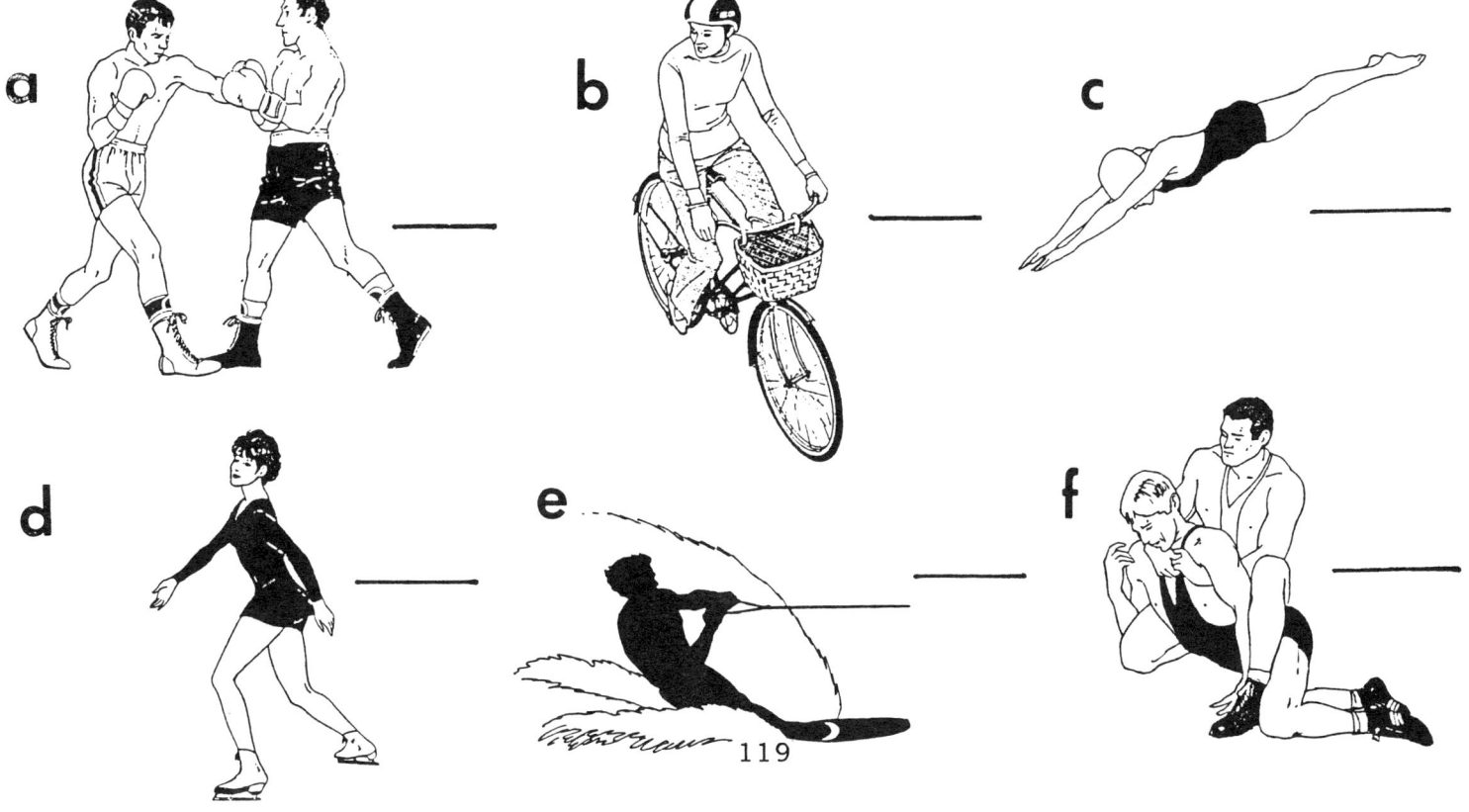

LEISURE

SPEAKING   CONVERSATION WITH A PARTNER

PART A.

Your conversation partner is a very interesting person. Find out what he/she likes to do during his/her leisure time. Record his/her answers on the lines.

    Ejemplo: Pregúntale: ¿Cuál es tu libro favorito?

1. libro _____

2. película _____

3. programa de televisión _____

4. el deporte que miras _____

5. el deporte que juegas _____

6. ¿Qué haces después de las clases? _____

7. ¿Qué haces durante el fin de semana? _____

Now that you have interviewed your partner. Write a paragraph about him/her based on the information you wrote down above.

_____
_____
_____
_____

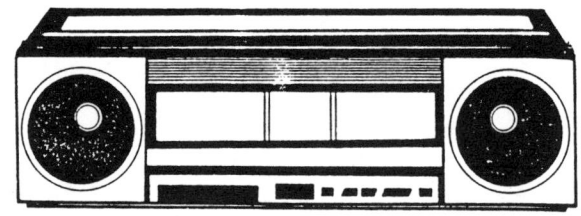

LEISURE

READING

PART A.

Read the advertisement for the concert. Answer the questions on the following page.

Gloria Estefan
MIAMI SOUND MACHINE

UNA CANTANTE MARAVILLOSA

INVITADO ESPECIAL

CHAS ELSTNER

Empieza su primera gira en España el 20 de agosto a las 8 de la noche y el 21 de agosto a las 8:30.

LOS BOLETOS EN VENTA

LUNES, EL 6 de agosto

En el Estadio Municipal de Barcelona

O para reservar los asientos por 25.000 pesetas
llame: 204 23 75 98

LEISURE

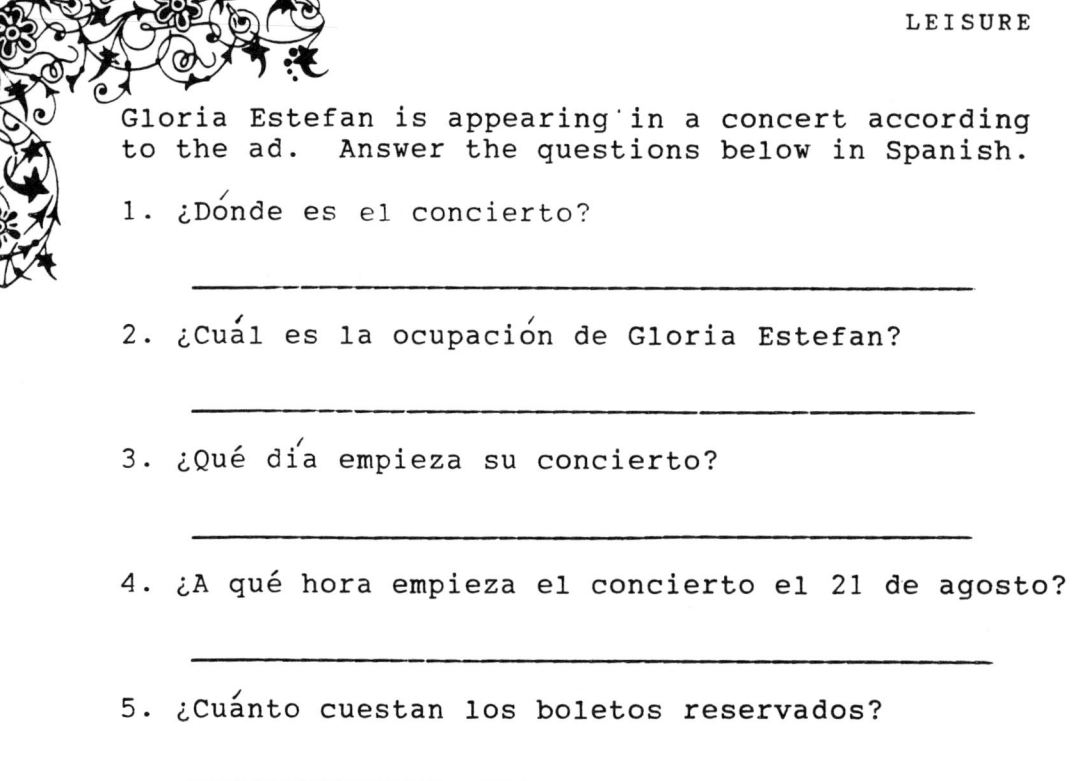

Gloria Estefan is appearing in a concert according to the ad. Answer the questions below in Spanish.

1. ¿Dónde es el concierto?

   _____

2. ¿Cuál es la ocupación de Gloria Estefan?

   _____

3. ¿Qué día empieza su concierto?

   _____

4. ¿A qué hora empieza el concierto el 21 de agosto?

   _____

5. ¿Cuánto cuestan los boletos reservados?

   _____

READING   LEISURE

PART B.

The World Cup Soccer Tournament is very important in the world of sports. Read the following article to find out who was victorious and other interesting information

DEPORTES

☆ ☆ ☆

LA COPA MUNDIAL 1990

EL XIV CAMPEONATO MUNDIAL DE FÚTBOL

EN ITALIA

FUE DEL 8 DE JUNIO AL 8 DE JULIO

　　Los jugadores famosos del mundo como Diego Maradona de la Argentina jugaron contra los equipos de Italia y Alemania Federal. Al final, los alemanes triunfaron y los argentinos tomaron el segundo puesto. Los italianos se quedaron con el tercer puesto del torneo.

　　Cuando el guardameta argentino, Sergio Goycoechea, regresó a su pueblo de Zárate, el alcalde lo declaró el **ciudadano ilustre** de Zárate. Era testimonio de su brillante actuación en el Campeonato Mundial de Fútbol.

Answer the following questions according to the article.

1. Where were the championship games played?_____

2. How many championships have been played?_____

3. What is the nationality of Diego Maradona?_____

4. Who were the winners of the World Cup games?_____

5. What place did Italy finish? _____

6. What honor was given to the Argentine goalie? _____
_____

READING

LEISURE

PART C.

Read the Spanish TV Guide below. Then indicate on what channel and at what time you would watch the programs listed below. (There may be more than one answer)

● Teleguía ●

TVE 1

15,00: TELEDIARIO

15,30: EL TIEMPO

15,35: DOCUMENTAL. El mundo bajo del mar de Cousteau

16,35: CORRUPCIÓN EN MIAMI. Programa policíaca norteamericana.

TVE 2

14,00: CURSO DE INGLÉS.

15,00: ITALIA 90. -FÚTBOL. Cuartos de Final. Desde el Estadio Comunale de Florencia. En directo.

17,00: VIDEOMIX. Videos musicales.

17,20: PELÍCULA. <<La noche del cometa>> 1984. EE.UU. 95 minutos. Director: Thom Eberhardt. Ciencia ficción.

ANTENA 3

15,30: HASTA LA MERIENDA. Dibujos Animados. <<Jem, chica pop>>. <<Transformers>>.

17,30: LA RULETA DE LA FORTUNA Concurso.

18,00: TELENOTICIAS.

18,20: CINE ESPAÑOL. <<Once pares de botas>> de Francisco Rovira Beleta, 1954, 96 minutos

TELECINCO 5

17,05: TELECUPÓN. Sorteo de la lotería.

17,20: LOVING. Telenovela norteamericana.

18,55: EL TRIBU DE LOS BRADY Comedia norteamericana.

19,25: CINE CORAZÓN. <<El chofer y la señora Daisy>>. 1989. Una historia sentimental.

TELEMADRID 7 ☆

15,00: LAS NUEVAS AVENTURAS DE POPEYE. Dibujos animados.

16,20: TENIS. Torneo de Wimbledon

18,00: IBIZA 90. Concierto de los Rolling Stones.

20,30: ESTRENOS TV. <<Viernes el trece>>. EE.UU. Película de terror.

	la cadena	la hora
An American Science Fiction Movie	_____	_____
The Weather Forecast	_____	_____
Cartoons	_____	_____
Music Videos	_____	_____
A Concert	_____	_____
A Horror Movie	_____	_____
The News	_____	_____
A Sports Event	_____	_____
A Crime Series	_____	_____
A Soap Opera	_____	_____

LEISURE

WRITING IN SPANISH

PART A.

You and your friends are planning to go to the movies. List four kinds of movies you can see.

_____
_____
_____
_____

PART B.

You are going to the Olympics. List five sports events you would like to see.

_____
_____
_____
_____
_____

PART C.

You have just returned from visiting your pen pal in Madrid. Write a thank you note to him/her mentioning where you went and what you did while you were there.

Muchas Gracias

LEISURE (TV & MOVIES)

ACROSS CLUES
1. soap operas
3. star
6. science fiction
8. funny
9. a western movie: una pelicula del
10. movie theater
14. horror movie: una pelicula de...
15. commercial
16. documentary

DOWN CLUES
2. news
4. cartoons
5. police movie: una pelicula...
7. musical
8. channel
11. romantic
12. movie (film)
13. sports

SPEAKING SITUATIONS

LEISURE

In pairs, prepare the conversations by playing roles as indicated in the situations.

You meet a friend outside at the end of the school day. Talk about where each of you are going and what you will do.

You and a friend are about to watch television. He/she suggests a program. Disagree and tell why.

Convince your friend to see a movie you just saw.

Your sister is playing in a soccer game. Invite your friend and make plans to go together.

PUBLIC SERVICES

AIMS

You will be able to...

- read and understand directions to use a pay phone. 
- talk on the phone.
- make a long distance phone call.
- read a telephone guide.
- write a friendly letter.
- talk to postal workers.

PUBLIC SERVICES

LISTENING

PART A

You and your friend Javier are at a café in Spain. You decide to call your friend Pepe. You go to the pay phone at the café, but you do not know how to use it. Javier tells you what to do. Listen carefully to the instructions for using a public telephone that will be read twice to you. After each step is read, write the number of the statement next to the appropriate picture.

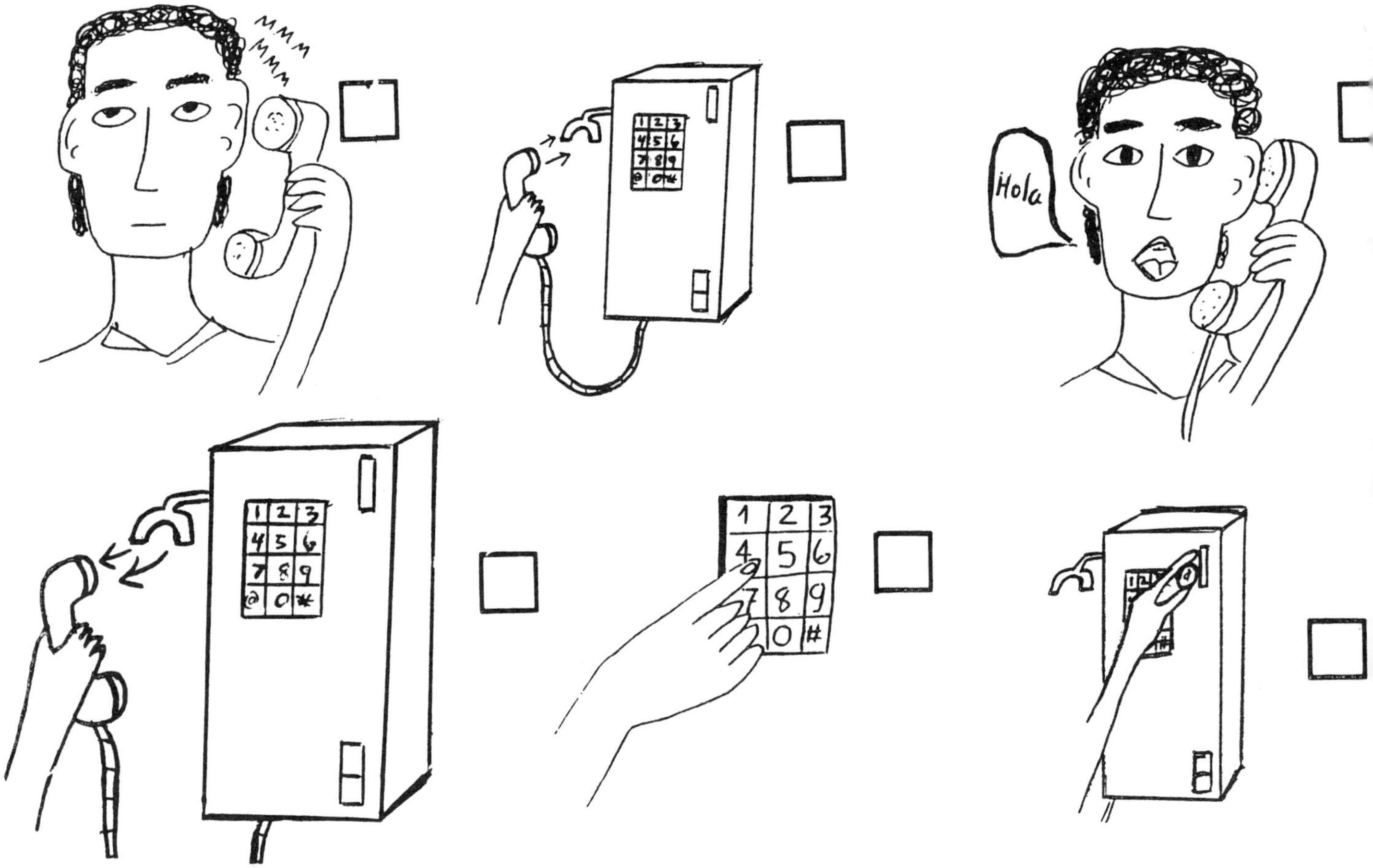

PART B.

You are at a party with a few friends and hear different parts of their conversations. Decide whether they are talking about the telephone company or the postal service. Listen carefully to the statements that will be read twice to you and check the appropriate box.

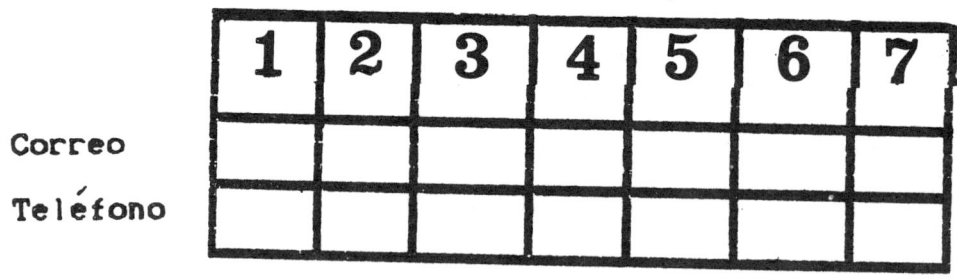

	1	2	3	4	5	6	7
Correo							
Teléfono							

CONVERSATION WITH A PARTNER

PUBLIC SERVICES

SPEAKING

PART A

You are on vacation in Spain and want to send a letter home to your parents. At the post office, you must have a conversation with the postal employee.

Working with your conversation partner, create a dialogue between the customer and the postal employee by using some of the following phrases and by adding some of your own.

Write a Spanish dialogue on the lines below and practice it with your partner.

el empleado
el cliente
la carta
por correo aéreo
Aquí lo tiene.

¿En qué puedo servirle?
Quisiera mandar...
¿Cómo quiere mandarla?
¿Cuánto cuesta?

_____
_____
_____
_____
_____
_____
_____
_____
_____
_____

PUBLIC SERVICES

On the following page you will find a page of advertisements from a telephone directory. Use it for Parts B and C.

PART B.

You are in Buenos Aires. You do not have a telephone book. Call the operator to get the phone numbers of the following places: a restaurant, a clothing store, a dance club, a shoe store, a pool, and a hotel. One of you will play the role of the operator.

PART C.

Read the following ads from a telephone directory in your hotel. With your partner, discuss where you would like to go this afternoon.

Pick four of the six places advertised and put a check next to your choices.

Then, taking turns playing the role of customer and store clerk, call each store for some pertinent information. You may ask what hours they are open, if reservations are necessary, or if they have a certain brand (marca) or item that you need.

Ejemplo: 1. ¡Hola! La tienda Confetti.

2. ¿Venden Uds. vestidos formales?

1. Sí, señorita. De muchas marcas.

2. ¿Cuánto cuestan?

1. Tengo muchos por 12.000 pesetas.

2. ¿Dónde está la tienda?

1. Está cerca del museo de arte.

CONVERSATION WITH A PARTNER
PARTS B and C

PISCINA MUNICIPAL DE BUENOS AIRES

diversion para toda la familia

abierto todos los días de 8-2 y de 4-6

llama por más información
26 87 51

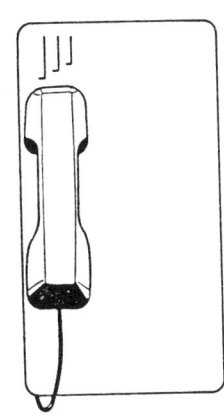

hotel El Porteño

50 habitaciones
aire acondicionado
taberna

reservaciones:
64 98 32

VENGAN A LA PLATA

el mejor lugar para bailar

para mayores de 16 años

abierto viernes y sábados

Metro Recoletos 3
Telef: 76 54 90

restaurante EL CHURRASCO

cocina típica argentina y tango

c/Florida 200
capital

reserve su mesa
Tel 55 74 86

CONFETTI

ropa para cualquier ocasión, ropa casual, deportiva, elegante.

abierto l-v
9-2, 5-9

Avenida 9 de Julio 44
Tel 24 65 78

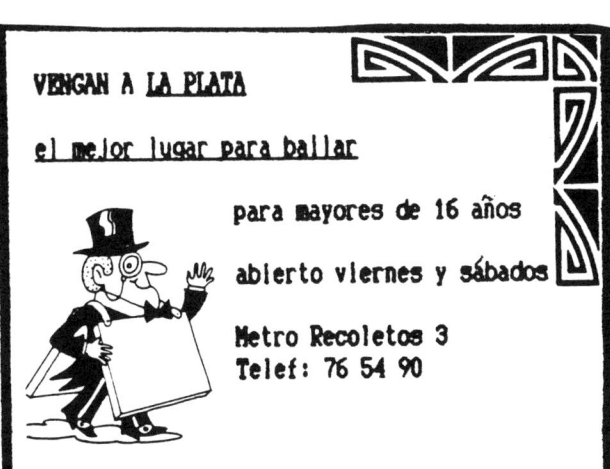

ZAPATOS LOS ANGELES

zapatos para toda ocasión importados y nacionales

Centro Comercial Moya
B.A.   Tel 49 87 02

PUBLIC SERVICES

READING

PART A.

Read this envelope and answer the questions below.

```
Srta. Maripaz Montalbán
calle Hospital, 32
Valencia 46003, España
```

```
Sr. Héctor Ramos
Avenida del Puerto, 56
San José   011200,
     Costa Rica
```

por correo aéreo

1. ¿Cuál es el remitente? _____

2. ¿Cuál es el código postal de Maripaz? _____

3. ¿Cuál es la dirección de Héctor? _____

4. ¿En qué país vive él? _____

5. ¿Cuánto cuestan los sellos? _____

6. ¿Cómo mandó la carta? _____

PUBLIC SERVICES

PART B.

Read this advertisement from a Spanish magazine and decide if the statements that follow are true or false.

ESPANATEL anuncia nuevas tarifas para llamadas de larga distancia. Ahorre dinero cuando Ud. hace una llamada a otros países. Recibe un descuento de 20% entre las cinco de la tarde y las diez de la noche los sábados y los domingos.

Circle the correct answers.

1. This is an ad from the telephone company.   True   False

2. You can get 20% off on local calls.   True   False

3. To receive a discount, you must make a long distance call between 5:00 and 10:00 p.m.   True   False

4. This service is available everyday.   True   False

PART C

Read this ad from a Venezuelan newspaper. Then answer the questions below in English.

CorreoVen anuncia la nueva serie de sellos de Simón Bolívar para conmemorar el cumpleaños de "El Libertador". La serie vendrá en denominaciones de 10 Bs., 20 Bs. y 30 Bs. Serán disponibles el 15 de noviembre en la casa de correos de su barrio.

1. Why are these new stamps being issued?_____

2. How much will the stamps be worth? _____

3. When will they be available?_____

4. Where can you buy them?_____

PUBLIC SERVICES

WRITING

PART A.

Your Spanish speaking friend, who is visiting you, is going shopping. You want him to call you when he is ready to come home so you can pick him up. Since he is unfamiliar with the pay phones in the United States, write a list of five steps he will need to know in order to make a pay phone call.

1. _____
2. _____
3. _____
4. _____
5. _____

PART B.

You are on vacation in Peru and want to write a letter and send a package home. Make a list of five items you will need.

1. _____
2. _____
3. _____
4. _____
5. _____

PART C.

You have just bought an answering machine. Write down the message you want to leave on the machine in order to practice it before you record it.

_____
_____
_____
_____

PUBLIC SERVICES

PART D.

You see this ad for summer employment in the newspaper. Write a letter in Spanish to the employer telling her why you are qualified for the job.

> Necesito jóvenes para trabajar en un restaurante. Buscamos camareros,-as. No necesita experiencia. Escríbanos a:
> Restaurante El Gaucho
> Calle Mendoza 32
> Santiago, Chile

_____
_____
_____
_____
_____
_____
_____
_____

PUBLIC SERVICES
SOPA DE LETRAS

Give the Spanish equivalent of the following words. Then find them in the puzzle. Circle the words from left to right, right to left, up or down, or diagonally. You may not use any word twice.

OPERATOR _____	ADDRESS _____
FAREWELL _____	DEAR _____
GREETING _____	AIRMAIL _____
ATTENTIVELY _____	A CALL _____
POST CARD _____	CITY _____
PHONE BOOTH _____	TOKEN _____
TO CONNECT _____	EMPLOYEE _____
CUSTOMER _____	STAMP _____
STAMP _____	TO SEND _____
TO SEND _____	DIGA (SP) _____
GUIDE _____	COIN SLOT _____
COIN _____	TO STAND ON LINE _____
LETTER _____	TO ASK FOR _____
TO SAY, TELL _____	

137

PUBLIC SERVICES
SPEAKING SITUATIONS

In pairs, prepare the conversation playing the roles indicated in the situation.

> You are making a phone call to your friend but he/she is not home. Leave a message with his/her mother.

> You want to buy stamps to mail some letters. Go to the post office and talk to the postal worker.

> Your friend has just written a letter. Find out to whom and why he/she has written the letter.

> Your friend from El Salvador feels homesick. He/She wants to write a letter to his/her family. Persuade him/her to call home.

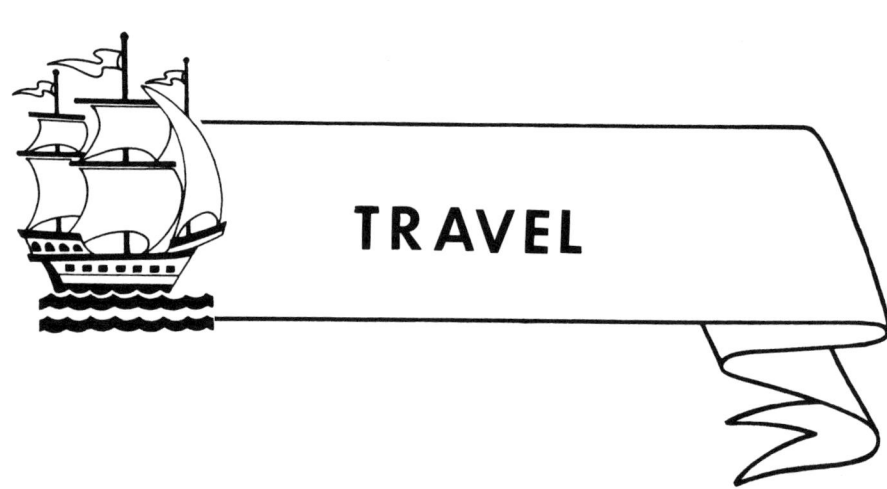

TRAVEL

AIMS

You will be able to...

- identify different ways of traveling.
- arrange for travel and hotel accomodations.
- read a travel ticket, travel brochures and a travel schedule.
- fill out simple travel forms.
- express your preferences and reactions about traveling.

TRAVEL

LISTENING

PART A

Are you a good detective? Find out how each person is traveling. Listen carefully to the passages that will be read twice to you and choose the means of transportation being described. Write the letter of your choice in the box.

PART B.

You are at an airport and need some flight information. Write the answers to the following questions based on the loud-speaker announcements you hear (statements read to you twice by your teacher) and the information you see on the schedule board below.

```
         AEROPUERTO DE BARAJAS (MADRID)

LLEGADAS                             SALIDAS
DE          VUELO   HORA   PUERTA    A              VUELO   HORA   PUERTA

Caracas      120    1700     3       Nueva York      452    1710     2
Los Ángeles  726    1705     7       México D.F.     817    1715     4
Lima         625    1712     8       Buenos Aires    315    1720     5
Santiago     528    1714    10       Santo Domingo   912    1725     6
```

1. ¿Cuál es el número de este vuelo? _____

2. ¿Cuál es el destino de este vuelo? _____

3. ¿A qué hora llega este vuelo? _____

4. ¿A qué puerta debe Ud. ir? _____

5. ¿De dónde es este vuelo? _____

TRAVEL

CONVERSATION WITH A PARTNER

SPEAKING

PART A

You and your partner play the roles of flight attendant and tourist. The person playing the role of the tourist questions the flight attendant to find out details about the flight, route of flight, airport of destination, weather at destination, etc.

PART B.

You and your partner play the roles of tourist and ticket agent at a train station. The tourist must find out information about the next departure to Madrid, time of departure, cost of the ticket, time of arrival in Madrid, and where to board the train.

PART C.

You and your partner play the roles of a hotel receptionist and a hotel guest who is registering. The receptionist must fill out the following form by interviewing the tourist.

Hotel Villa Real

FECHA_____

NOMBRE Y APELLIDO_____

DIRECCIÓN_____

PAÍS_____   NACIONALIDAD_____

NÚMERO DE PERSONAS_____   FECHA LLEGADA_____
                           FECHA SALIDA_____

NÚMERO DE LLAVES DESEADOS_____   IDENTIFICACIÓN_____

<u>PREFERENCIA DE HABITACIÓN(ES)</u>:   PREFERENCIA DE PISO_____

_____ cerca del ascensor
_____ cerca de la piscina
_____ habitación no fumar
_____ con baño privado
_____ con sauna privada
_____ terraza
_____ vista a la calle
_____ aire acondicionado
_____ con cocina

**** BIENVENIDOS ****

TRAVEL

READING

PART A.

I. Answer the questions based on what you read on this travel ticket.

	BILLETE PLAZAS SENTADAS Y LITERAS No. 499742	

PASAJEROS: SR./SRA. PIÑEDA
2 ASIENTOS
de   MADRID CHAMARTIN hasta VALENCIA

SALIDA: EL 21.03.90   HORA 8.42   TREN 313
LLEGADA   15.48

NO FUMADOR   CLASE 2a   COCHE 43   ASIENTOS 24y27   PRECIO 5900 PTS

1. ¿Cómo viajan? _____
2. ¿Cuánto vale este billete? _____
3. ¿Cuántas personas viajan? _____
4. ¿De dónde salen? _____
5. ¿A qué hora llega? _____

PART B.

Read this travel ad from a Spanish newspaper. Then answer the questions below in English.

VENGA A LOS PIRINEOS ESTE VERANO

con su agencia de viajes La Española, ¡usted recibe mas!

Uds. pueden hacer un viaje con nosotros.
** Nosotros les hacemos las reservaciones.

Los Pirineos están en el norte de España en la frontera entre Francia y España. Estas montañas son bonitas todo el año. Hay que verlas.

En los Pirineos se puede ...

... ver los puntos de interés

... ir de camping

... alquilar una moto

Hay vuelos que salen de Nueva York todos los días.

Llámenos. 55.45.67

---

1. What are Los Pirineos? _____

2. Where are they located? _____

3. According to this ad, what are three activities you can do there?

    a. _____

    b. _____

    c. _____

PART C.   TRAVEL

Read the following reduced far information and answer the questions below in English.

> TARJETA VERDE
>
> 50%
>
> DE DESCUENTO
>
>
>
> PARA LAS MUJERES A PARTIR DE LOS 60 AÑOS Y PARA LOS HOMBRES A PARTIR DE LOS 65 AÑOS
>
> HAY QUE VIAJAR EN SEGUNDA CLASE EN TODOS LOS TRENES
>
> CON ESTA OFERTA SOLO TIENE QUE PAGAR UN SUPLEMENTO EN TALGO
>
> SE PUEDE OBTENER ESTA TARJETA EN LA ESTACIÓN DE FERROCARRIL O EN LA AGENCIA DE VIAJES

1. What means of transportation is being discussed? _____

2. Name two restrictions on this ticket. _____

3. Where can this card be purchased? _____

For what means of transportation is this ticket? _____

When was this ticket valid? _____

TRAVEL

PART D.

Write the appropriate word that the picture expresses on the line under the picture. A list of Spanish words is provided below.

_____   _____   _____

_____   _____   _____

_____   _____   _____

PLAYA   RESTAURANTE   LAGO   PISCINA

ACCESO PARA LAS PERSONAS INVÁLIDAS   CANCHAS DE ESQUÍ

AIRE ACONDICIONADO   PRIMERA CLASE   FUMADORES

WRITING

PART A.

You are going to the airport and want to be sure that you have everything you need for your vacation. In Spanish, write a list six items you will need to carry with you to the airport.

_____ _____
_____
_____
_____
_____
_____

PART B.

You and your family are traveling by car on vacation in Mexico. At the moment, you are in Guaymas, a beach resort. Write a message in Spanish, on the post card below, to a friend describing your vacation and your travel arrangements.

```
┌─────────────────────────────────────────────────────┐
│ GUAYMAS una vista panorámica                        │
│ del Mar de Cortéz                 ┌──────┐          │
│                                   │ sello│          │
│                                   └──────┘          │
│                     TARJETA POSTAL                  │
│                            │                        │
│                            │                        │
│                            │  NOMBRE_____   │
│                            │  DIRECCIÓN_____   │
│                            │  _____   │
│                            │  _____   │
│                            │           _____     │
│                            │            PAÍS        │
└─────────────────────────────────────────────────────┘
```

TRAVEL

PART C.

You and your friends are discussing vacation plans. Write a list of five means of transportation in Spanish.

PART D.

You are traveling in an airplane on the way to a vacation at your uncle's farm in the Dominican Republic. Before landing at the Aeropuerto Internacional de la Republica Dominicana in Santo Domingo, fill out this form for Customs in Spanish.

```
           DECLARACIÓN DE ADUANAS

   Todo viajero debe facilitar la información siguiente

   1. Nombre_____
           apellido      nombre      segundo nombre

   2. Dirección_____
                            calle

   _____
   pueblo      estado           código postal

   _____
   país

   fecha de nacimiento _____/_____/_____
                         mes    día    año

   línea aérea y número del vuelo_____

   _____
        firma           fecha (mes/día/año)
```

147

TRAVEL CRUCIGRAMA

Complete the crossword puzzle below in Spanish.

ACROSS CLUES

2. You make this at a hotel
7. schedule
8. she serves food on an airplane
9. departure
10. someone who travels
12. ticket
13. boat
16. someone who flies an airplane
18. suitcase
19. room
22. you need this to board a plane
23. you take these with a camera

DOWN CLUES

1. flight
3. luggage
4. customs
5. tourist
6. passport
11. souvenirs
14. to rent
15. taxi
17. plane
18. subway
20. seat
21. train

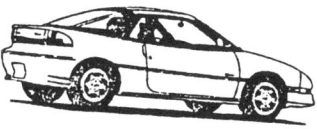

TRAVEL
SPEAKING SITUATIONS

In pairs, prepare the conversation playing the roles indicated in the situation.

1. It is vacation time. Your parents want to stay home and you would like to travel. Convince them to go on a trip.

2. You are planning a trip to see Carnaval in Miami. Speak with a travel agent and make the arrangements for this trip.

3. You are taking a bus ride to Tijuana. You are seated next to a person your age from Mexico. Start a conversation with him/her.

4. You are on tour in San Juan, Puerto Rico and your bus breaks down. Your guide suggests waiting at a local hotel until the bus is repaired. React unfavorably and suggest another means of transportation.